More Discussion Starters

More Discussion Starters

Activities for Building Speaking Fluency

Keith S. Folse, Ph.D.

M.A. TESOL Program
University of Central Florida

Jeanine Ivone

English Language Institute
University of South Florida

Ann Arbor
THE UNIVERSITY OF MICHIGAN PRESS

For my good friend Michael Tinsley, who always encourages me to write. KF

For my dad, who believes in me when I don't believe in myself. JI

Acknowledgments

We would like to thank those teachers who helped in the field-testing of the material in this text, especially Paula Blum and Susan Reynolds. In addition, we are indebted to Mary Goodman for her help in locating sources for Unit 2.

We would also like to thank the staff at the University of Michigan Press who have been instrumental in the success of the Discussion Starters series, namely, Kelly Sippell, Mary Erwin, Chris Milton, and Giles Brown.

Library of Congress, Prints and Photographs Division for Jimmy Carter, LC-USZ62-13039 DLC; Hillary Clinton, LC-USZ62-107702 DLC; John F. Kennedy, LC-USZ62-117124 DLC; and Eleanor Roosevelt, LC-USZ62-25812 DLC.

Contents

To the Teacher   xi

Advice from the Authors to the Students   xix

Unit

1   Predicting the Future   1

2   You Can Be the Judge: Who Is the Real Owner?   10

3   Cell Phones   16

4   An Interviewer's Ideal Person to Interview   25

5   Jokes: Is It Funny? Culture and Humor   30

6   Proverbs   39

7   Put the Story Together: The Patient   44

8   Life after Death?   46

9   Finish the Story: The Young Boy's Dilemma   53

10 The Death Penalty   56

11 Put the Story Together: The Great Beyond   70

12 The Punishment and the Crime   72

13 Corporal Punishment   78

14 Who Should Control Your Safety?   88

15 More Practice with Proverbs   99

16 Faith Healing: Trust the Doctor or Trust God?   104

17 The Abortion Debate   111

18 Put the Story Together: A Van Full of Penguins   121

19 The 10 Most Important Events in History   124

20 Playing God: Genetic Engineering   132

Communication Activities   141

Answer Key for Language Review Exercises   159

To the Teacher

Teaching Discussion Classes

One of the most challenging teaching situations is a discussion or speaking class. In theory, the teacher (or a student) can bring up a given topic and the students will discuss its merits or controversial aspects. In reality, however, this is rarely the case. In most classes, the most confident students tend to dominate the discussion and the weaker students, those who really need the class, quickly withdraw. In order to keep the "discussion" going, the teacher ends up trying to draw the students out. In effect, this "discussion" often becomes a question and answer exchange between the teacher and a few students.

With a wide variety of engaging topics and unique interactive exercises designed to keep the discussion flowing, *More Discussion Starters* aims to balance the speaking loads of all the students in the class and thus promote an environment in which everyone has not only a chance but a real need to speak out. In fact, many times the exercises have been designed so that the students cannot complete the speaking task unless everyone in the group participates and speaks up. Therefore, students actually need the input of other students to complete the discussion task.

Using the Book

The most important pedagogical point involved in using this book is that the teacher give the students the time and framework to think about their own ideas so they can form a coherent opinion. It is extremely important to realize that our students have a number of factors working against them: they may lack confidence in their English skills, they may not have any background information about the topic, they may not have participated in group discussion much, they may not be interested in the topic because they have not been engaged (personally), and they may not have any opinion at all about the topic (though this last factor is definitely not limited to nonnative speakers).

These possible limitations of our students have been taken into account, and the exercises within each unit are set up in a special way in order to help the students develop and organize their ideas and thus foster confidence in their knowledge of the topic, which will facilitate speaking. Whenever a question for discussion is introduced, there is a prerequisite exercise that has the students write out their own ideas. This exercise sometimes consists of a series of short questions designed to guide the students through the critical thinking process. At other times, the exercise has two or three questions that are more general in nature but still aim to guide the students so that they can put their ideas down on paper.

This book is built on the premise that having to write out our thoughts on paper forces us to reexamine, rethink, and recycle our ideas until we have a much neater package. At workshops, when teachers are asked their opinion about a topic and then told, before everyone has had a chance to speak out, to write out their opinions in 25 to 50 words, it is usually the case that their written opinions have changed somewhat from their original opinion. Certainly they are more directed and more to the point. When teachers are then asked to continue talking about the topic in question, the discussion seems to flow much better. In addition, teachers who were reluctant to speak up before now do so. The printed word in front of them seems to be an anchor for those who were hesitant or reluctant to speak up before. The simple act of writing about one's thoughts on paper before having to speak does make a real difference in not only the quality but also the quantity (fluency) of the discussion.

For example, when a student is suddenly confronted with the statement "People shouldn't drink and drive," it might be difficult for many students to say something that makes much sense and really expresses their true opinion. Most students in this situation in a group will be so nervous about what they are going to say that they can't and don't listen to the other students until after they themselves have spoken. Thus, what ensues more resembles a series of monologues than a dialogue or discussion of sorts. For this class to be a real learning and developing situation with interaction, it is much better—and we would argue necessary—to have the students write out their ideas briefly beforehand.

Topics for Discussion

A quick glance at the table of contents will reveal that the 20 units cover an extremely wide range of topics. Though most of the topics in the text are serious (corporal punishment and abortion), many others deal with lighter topics (humor and culture). The topics were chosen because they are of interest to our student base. In addition, topics that may become dated very quickly were not included.

Unlike other books on the market today, *More Discussion Starters* does not use imaginary situations for discussion (e.g., "Imagine that you won the lottery"). When people have been challenged to come up with a potential solution to a task or problem, they rightfully expect to be able to hear what the "correct" answer is. For example, in the numerous court cases mentioned in this book, there is always a real court judgment given by a real judge or real jury. After the students have discussed each other's verdicts and supporting reasons, they are then (and only then!) instructed to turn to the back of the book to discover the actual decision of the judge or the jury.

The activities, tasks, and topics chosen for this book are real situations from all over the world. When students are asked what they would do in a given situation, there is a real answer that is provided.

Types of Interaction in the Exercises

Most of the units in this book introduce a problem or controversial topic at the beginning of the unit. This is then followed by a series of exercises designed to prepare all of the students so that they can express their ideas at the next class meeting. A unit usually includes several kinds of oral fluency activities, but some of the major types of activities are listed here.

Problem-solving tasks: A unique feature of this text is that *every* unit in this text has several tasks in which students must cooperate to solve a problem while using English.

Court cases: Exercises in Units 2, 3, 10, 12, 13, 16, 17. Each of these exercises pertains to a real court case that involves the topic of the unit. Students are told to work out their own solution as if they were the judge or jury and then discuss their ideas later in class. Actual decisions are revealed in the communication activities at the back of the book.

Finish the story: Unit 9. A story that has a unique ending has been begun in the unit, but the ending has deliberately been left off. Instructions are given for having students discuss possible endings and reasons for their choices. As with all the material in this text, an actual story has been used.

Role play: Units 2, 4, 10, 14, 16, 17. Though the unit does not revolve around the role-play exercise, these units do include an exercise that has the students do some sort of role play regarding the topic of the unit. Possible roles are often suggested, but it is up to the teacher to choose which roles should be used. In addition, some role plays include directions for differing numbers of students (e.g., if there are four students, do these communication activities, but if there are six students, do these other communication activities). Whether or not role plays succeed in class depends a lot on the dynamics of the given group of students.

Charts, scales, and questionnaires: Units 1, 3, 5, 8, 9, 10, 12, 14, 16, 17, 19, 20. Students must work together to complete information in a chart or questionnaire. Since each student has only a piece of the information in a given chart, it is necessary that all students speak up in the activity for the group to be able to complete the chart successfully. Questionnaires actively engage the students at a personal level; later on, students compare their responses with responses of other students in their groups.

Discussion and oral presentations: Units 1, 4, 5, 6, 10, 14, 15, 19. Though these units contain other types of interaction, one of the main points of these units is that students compile information to present to the rest of the class.

Put the story together: Units 7, 11, 18. Students work in large groups to solve a strip story. Each student has one piece of the story, and all students must work together or a solution is impossible.

Small group discussions: Units 1, 2, 3, 4, 5, 6, 8, 9, 10, 12, 13, 14, 15, 16, 17, 19, 20. One of the main features of these units is an exercise that fosters active interaction among the members of a small group (three to five students).

Text Organization

More Discussion Starters consists of 20 self-contained units. There is ample background material in the text to start students on their way to a discussion. Teachers do not have to spend time searching for newspaper or magazine articles that most of the students in the class will be able to comprehend (which is in itself a major job for any teacher), and students do not have to do extensive outside reading in order to feel qualified to talk about the topics. Thus, students can spend their class time speaking about and discussing topics rather than reading them silently. (Naturally, teachers may assign additional readings to supplement the topics in *More Discussion Starters* if they wish.)

An important unique feature of this text is that there are efficient, that is, simple yet effective, homework exercises in which students must sort out their ideas and opinions before coming to class to discuss or talk about the issues in the textbook. This allows all students to be prepared for the speaking activities in class and is of special importance to the weaker, less confident nonnative speakers. It also allows the teacher to feel confident that all the students in the class, regardless of their native country, education level, or age, now have a known common background about the topic. Some students will naturally know more about certain topics, but now the teacher at least has a common denominator from which to start discussion.

Each unit contains a number of exercises that provide speaking interaction about a central topic or idea. In most of these activities, students must work together in pairs or small groups to solve a problem, reach a consensus, discuss ideas, or complete some other kind of speaking task.

A particular strength of the design of this text is that there is no set pattern for introducing a topic. Units begin with illlustrations, questionnaires, court cases, and proverbs. This variety should keep a discussion course from becoming monotonous or too predictable after a few weeks.

Sequencing of Topics (units)

There is no one best way of sequencing the units or topics in this book. All units are independent of each other. Thus, the class could begin with any of the units and then continue with any other unit.

As much as possible, the difficulty level in the units is consistent. What is different, however, is the topic of the units. Thus, one of the few factors that might influence the "best" sequencing of units for a given group of students is the topics themselves.

The topics in the units have been included because they lend themselves to discussion. This means of course that some of these topics are controversial. If the topics were not controversial or would not naturally elicit a variety of opinions, they would not be good discussion starters. One way to lessen the chance of "forcing" a controversial topic on a group of students is to have the students themselves choose which units they would like to cover in the course. It is recommended that the teacher choose one unit to begin the term and that one of the students' first assignments be to get into small groups of three to five students and rank the topics (i.e., units) in the textbook in terms of which units they would like to do first. This has numerous benefits for the class. First, the teacher is no longer dictating the course. Second, the students have a stronger sense of community. Third, this task itself requires speaking and negotiating practice using spoken English. Finally, students are more likely to have better discussions if they are interested in the topics.

Communication Activities

At the back of this text, there are 91 communication activities. These are an essential part of almost every unit. In a given exercise in a unit, students are often told to work in pairs or small groups. Student A will be told to look at one communication activity while student B will be told to look at another communication activity. In this way, the students hold different pieces of information that only they know and that they must share verbally with their partner. Since the two pieces of information are not on the same page or even near each other in the text, the students must talk to their partners to complete the given language task.

It is essential that students understand the whole activity before teachers have students do the communication activities. The teacher should give an overview of the exercise, explain how the communication task will work, divide the class into pairs or groups as the exercise instructions indicate, and then walk around the room to help any student who might still have questions.

Fluency versus Accuracy in Language Learning

All exercises that are done in any language class are done either for accuracy, for fluency, or for a combination of the two. However, we teachers very often tend to do one to the exclusion of the other, and much of what we do, especially what we have traditionally done, is heavily oriented toward accuracy. While this may be appropriate at lower levels of language proficiency, there is a need to balance accuracy exercises with fluency exercises.

For an exercise to be fluency oriented, the exercise should be slightly below the actual level of the students so that the student can practice extensively without becoming too distracted by difficult or unfamiliar vocabulary and grammatical points. In other words, the students should find the language level in the exercise easy. The purpose of a fluency exercise is to increase the volume of actual language practice that students can accomplish in the given time limitations. Having the students write out their opinions ahead of time, as many of the exercises require, will allow the students to concentrate their efforts in class on actual speaking rather than on reading, listening, or vocabulary. Students will learn to speak about a topic in English by doing just that—actually spending class time speaking.

Integrated Skills

Having students write something on the topic before they discuss the topic is innovative and integrates writing and speaking. Although this book is designed primarily to encourage speaking, it calls for other skills such as reading, writing, listening, working in groups, and cooperative learning, yet this is accomplished without students having to do an extensive amount of outside reading or writing, which allows the students to focus on the primary goal of this text—speaking fluency and discussion skills.

Vocabulary Development

Regardless of any ESL or EFL student's level, vocabulary development is one of the primary concerns of many students. To help students acquire and retain important new vocabulary that pertains to the topics presented in the units of *More Discussion Starters,* each unit concludes with a vocabulary check called Language Review. The format for this exercise varies from unit to unit. Examples of the different formats follow.

Key word
Read the key word (in bold) in the left column. Circle the letter of the choice that is related to the key word.

1. **split**   a. help   b. divide   c. decorate
2. **annual**   a. once a day   b. once a month   c. once a year

Completion
Use the vocabulary items in the box to complete the sentences.

feather	flock	brief	as long as	scratch

1. We wrote a _____ letter to the company to explain our situation.

2. _____ you take this medicine, you will be fine.

Definition
Match the definition in the right column with the correct word in the left column.

Vocabulary   *Definition*

____ 1. specialist   a. person who focuses on one particular area of study

____ 2. suffer   b. to put steady force on something

____ 3. press   c. to experience pain

Original explanations and production

1. Explain *used to* (e.g., "I used to hate onions, but now I love them").

_____

_____

_____

2. Make three sentences using *no longer.*

   a. _____

   b. _____

   c. _____

Providing synonyms and problem solving

These questions contain underlined words that are key vocabulary words that
you should remember. Write a synonym or definition for the vocabulary words
and then provide a logical answer to the questions.

1. If the police arrest you for drinking and then driving a car, this might result
   in the <u>suspension</u> of what?

   suspension   _____

   answer: _____

2. When was the last time that you were <u>outraged</u>?

   outraged   _____

   answer: _____

Web Sites for Further Study and Discussion

At the end of each unit, we have included a Web address that will direct you to
other sites that are related to the topic or topics covered in that unit. We realize that each group of students is different. Some students may need additional information on a given topic before they are ready to discuss the material. In
addition, students who want extra English practice can work on their reading
and vocabulary skills by perusing the Web sites. As with any Internet activity, we
recommend that the teacher visit each Web site to check out the contents first-
hand to make sure the material is suitable for the students. Because Internet
sites appear and disappear so quickly, if you have ideas for additional Web sites,
please send them to esladmin@umich.edu.

Answer Key

The answers for Language Review, the last exercise in each of the 20 units, are
provided at the back of the book. These answers are provided so that the students may check their own work. Logically, it is supposed that the students will
use the key <u>only</u> after they have actually completed the exercise. It is further
hoped that students will return to the exercise to detect the source of their
error to complete the learning process.

Advice from the Authors to the Students

We hope that you will enjoy the topics and activities in this book! Here are some tips and suggestions for using this book to improve your speaking skills in English.

Some people are naturally good at speaking about certain topics. The natural tendency of these extroverted people is to start a topic for discussion. These people have good skills in maintaining the discussion, too. Other people are more quiet and reserved. They may have many ideas to add to the topic, but their natural tendency is to listen. These introverted people are participating in the discussion, too, but in a different way. Regardless of your personality type, you CAN be an active participant in discussions in English. You CAN become a better speaker in English.

In order to improve your discussion skills in English, here are some tips that we strongly recommend.

1. Learn everything you can about the topic because people who are good discussion participants have solid background knowledge of the topic;
2. Learn the vocabulary associated with that topic because you cannot discuss a topic well if you do not know the basic vocabulary for that topic;
3. Learn to use key phrases that allow you to initiate topics (see examples on page xx);
4. Learn to use key phrases that allow you to maintain discussions (see examples on page xx);
5. Learn to use key phrases that make others talk because a discussion NEVER involves just you—without other people you have NO discussion (see examples on page xx);
6. Learn to be a good listener by showing respect for others in your group, which means that you should let everyone have the floor and you should not interrupt others;
7. Learn to be tolerant of others' ideas because it is this VARIETY of ideas that makes a discussion interesting;
8. Do all of the homework assignments in this book because research in foreign language studies shows that homework activities that require you to

write out your ideas will greatly improve the quality and quantity of the language that you produce in class discussions the next day.

Here are some examples of key phrases to use to improve discussion skills.

To initiate a discussion

- What do you think about _____?
- Do you think _____ is a good thing?
- This topic makes me mad. (explain why)
- I can't believe there are people who think . . . (Explain your position.)

To state your opinion

- I think _____ is a good thing.
- I don't think _____ is a good thing.

To maintain a discussion

- Are there any other ideas on _____ ?
- Who else agrees with (name)?
- Does anyone else have anything to add to what (name) just said?
- Can anyone else think of another reason to support this idea?
- You know, that's an interesting point that you've just made. (Offer your own opinion now.)

To bring someone else's ideas into the discussion

- (name), what do you think about _____ ?
- Does anyone else have anything to add?

To assess agreement

- OK, so how many people are in favor of _____ ?
- How many people agree with what (name) just said?
- OK, is this what the rest of you think, too?

To indicate agreement

- I agree with (name).
- I agree with what (name) just said.
- I think that's right. (Explain your own position now.)

To indicate disagreement in a polite way

- I understand what you (or name) are saying, but I think . . .
- I understand what you (or name) are saying, but I wonder if you have considered (another reason or another idea).
- Hmmm. . . . That's interesting, but I wonder if you have considered . . .

To contrast two views on an issue

- Most of us agree that the best decision is to _____ . What are some of the reasons that other people might have for disagreeing with this?
- OK, we've heard one side of the issue. What is the other side?

To summarize a discussion

- OK, we're almost out of time. Where do we stand on this topic?
- OK, so what is the consensus of our group?
- Do we have a consensus?
- It looks like we'll have to agree to disagree on this topic because our opinions are too far apart.

Predicting the Future

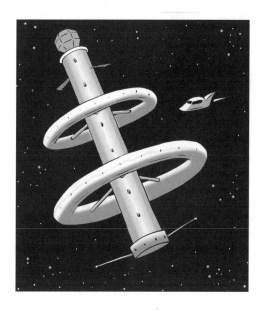

INTRODUCTION

What did our grandparents think the future would bring? What do you think the future will bring? What things will change the most in one hundred years? The topics in this unit deal with predictions for the future.

Exercise 1.1

Write the current year here: _____
Add 50 years: _____

How do you think life will be different 50 years from now? In 100–150 words, describe life 50 years from now. Give specific examples of how you think life will be different.

_____

_____

_____

_____

_____

_____

_____

_____

_____

_____

_____

Exercise 1.2

Work in small groups (three or four students). Take turns presenting your ideas about how life will be different in 50 years. It is important for everyone in the group to listen to everyone's ideas. If there is something that you do not understand, ask the speaker to repeat or explain what he or she said. After you listen to each speaker, write down the most interesting prediction from that speaker.

Student Name	The Most Interesting Prediction

Exercise 1.3

Here are some predictions about life 50 years from now. Read each of these predictions and circle the number to indicate how likely you believe each of these predictions is. Then write a sentence to explain your answer. Try to give good details, facts, or reasons to support your predictions.

Circle 1 if you believe the prediction is *very likely.*
Circle 2 if you believe the prediction is *likely.*
Circle 3 if you believe the prediction is *possible.*
Circle 4 if you believe the prediction is *unlikely (but possible).*
Circle 5 if you believe the prediction is *impossible.*

a. 1   2   3   4   5   People will no longer die from cancer.

_____

_____

_____

b. 1   2   3   4   5   We will use the same kind of cameras that we use now to take photographs.

_____

_____

_____

c. 1   2   3   4   5   Students will continue to use books in school.

_____

_____

_____

d. 1   2   3   4   5   English will be so popular that it will replace native languages in some countries.

_____

_____

_____

e. 1　2　3　4　5　　Cars will be the principal way that people travel daily.

_____

_____

_____

f. 1　2　3　4　5　　People will be able to eat anything, take a special pill, and not gain any weight.

_____

_____

_____

g. 1　2　3　4　5　　People will use email as the number one means of communication.

_____

_____

_____

h. 1　2　3　4　5　　Average citizens will be able to travel to the moon regularly.

_____

_____

_____

i. 1　2　3　4　5　　People will no longer use coins and paper money when they buy something.

_____

_____

_____

j. 1 2 3 4 5   AIDS will be the number one killer disease around the world.

_____

_____

_____

k. 1 2 3 4 5   Women will be more visible in politics. The United States will have a woman president.

_____

_____

_____

l. 1 2 3 4 5   No one will use telephones any more.

_____

_____

_____

m. 1 2 3 4 5   Garbage will be removed from our homes as it is now. (Trucks will come to pick up garbage that we put out in front of our houses in bags or cans.)

_____

_____

_____

n. 1 2 3 4 5   People will go to supermarkets to buy their food to cook.

_____

_____

_____

o. 1   2   3   4   5   Gays and lesbians will be able to marry legally.

_____

_____

_____

Exercise 1.4

Work in small groups. Compare your answers for the 15 situations in exercise 1.3 by telling which number you circled and then your reason for choosing this number.

Exercise 1.5

Comparing the Past, the Present, and the Future

Work in groups of three. Each student will prepare a brief report about the past, present, and future situation for a different topic, using the Communication Activities at the back of the book.

Step 1. Each student should look at one of these communication activities: 12, 31, 47, 64, 78, and 86.

Step 2. Write your communication activity number in the box and your topic on the line.

☐   General topic: _____

Step 3. Describe this topic in the past. What did people do? What did people do at an even earlier time?

Step 4. Describe this topic in the present. What do people do? What is usual?

Step 5. Describe this topic in the future. What will people do? What are people going to do?

THE PAST (*Grammar hint:* use past tense; use *used to;* use *could;* use negatives)

_____

_____

_____

_____

_____

_____

_____

_____

THE PRESENT (*Grammar hint:* use present tense; use *can, be able to;* use negatives)

_____

_____

_____

_____

_____

_____

_____

THE FUTURE (*Grammar hint:* use *will;* use *be going to;* use *may, might;* use negatives)

_____

_____

_____

_____

_____

_____

_____

Language Review

1. Explain *used to* (e.g., "I used to hate onions, but now I love them").

_____

_____

_____

_____

2. Make three sentences using *no longer.*

a. _____

b. _____

c. _____

3. Write two sentences that mean the same thing. In the first sentence, use the verb *predict.* In the second sentence, use the noun *prediction* to express the same meaning as in the first sentence.

_____

_____

4. Make a list of any new or difficult vocabulary that you found in this unit or in the classroom discussions from this unit. Write a brief definition and an example phrase or sentence. Ask your teacher to check your work.

a. _____ / _____

_____

_____

b. _____ / _____

_____

_____

c. _____ / _____

_____

_____

d. _____ / _____

_____

_____

e. _____ / _____

_____

_____

Be sure to visit <<u>www.press.umich.edu/esl</u>> for ideas on related Web sites, videos, and other activities.

You Can Be the Judge: Who Is the Real Owner?

INTRODUCTION

This unit deals with a simple but difficult problem. Two people claim that they own the same item. Only one person can be the rightful owner. What makes this case so special is that the real owner will gain one million dollars.

Exercise 2.1

Read this court case about determining ownership of a very important item.

It is common for companies to promote their products by having some sort of competition with large prizes. For example, a company might have a contest to see who can come up with the best slogan to promote a certain product. Another company might ask contestants to write in approximately 50 words why they prefer a particular product.

Soft-drink companies often have competitions that involve both small amounts of money and other prizes. However, Pepsi, a leading soft-drink company, recently had a competition with a very rich prize. To participate in this contest, people had to purchase a bottle of Pepsi and look under the cap on the bottle. Customers could win prizes ranging from a free soft drink to one million dollars!

Because of this contest, two workers in a health foods store recently had a problem regarding a Pepsi. Judy Richardson bought a Pepsi, which she left unopened in the refrigerator at work. Sindy Allen, a co-worker who worked the night shift, saw the soft drink in the refrigerator and decided to drink it. After opening it, Allen discovered that the bottle cap had the million-dollar prize.

Richardson says that the Pepsi was hers and that the million-dollar prize should be hers. Allen says that she found the Pepsi in the refrigerator at work and that there is no way to prove that it is Richardson's drink. She said that she was cleaning the refrigerator and asked if the Pepsi belonged to anyone. Richardson has no receipt for the soft drink. Former co-workers at the store testified that Richardson was practically addicted to Pepsi and that the area where Richardson left the soft drink was the spot where she usually kept her bottles of Pepsi.

Allen offered to split the money with Richardson, but Richardson refused. The winner of this contest would not get a lump sum of one million dollars but rather an annual payment of fifty thousand dollars for 20 years. The two women went to court when they could not resolve this issue amicably.

Exercise 2.2

If you were the judge, would you rule in favor of Richardson or in favor of Allen? _____

Why? Write two or three reasons for your decision. _____

_____

Exercise 2.3

Work in small groups. Discuss your decision and your reasons. When you finish, read communication activity 70 for the result of this case.

Exercise 2.4

Role Play

Work in small groups (four or six people). Each person should do ONE of the communication activities. If there are four people, do 3, 17, 32, and 49. If there are six people, do 3, 17, 32, 49, 65, and 89.

Step 1. What is your communication activity number? _____

Step 2. Write who you are on this line. _____

Step 3. What are your feelings about what happened? Why do you feel this way? Write your responses on these lines.

_____

_____

_____

_____

Step 4. Now work in groups. You are the person in step 2. Introduce yourself. Tell your opinion of the problem. Tell the group what you think should happen and why. Feel free to ask the other members questions or to comment on their statements during the discussion.

Exercise 2.5

Useful Proverbs and Sayings

Here are some sayings in English that are related to the details of this case. What does each mean? How could it be related to this case?

a. "Finders keepers, losers weepers."

Meaning: _____

_____

_____

_____

Relation to this case: _____

_____

_____

_____

_____

_____

b. "Do unto others as you would have them do unto you."

Meaning: _____

_____

_____

Relation to this case: _____

_____

_____

_____

_____

c. "Possession is 9/10 [nine-tenths] of the law."

Meaning: _____

_____

_____

Relation to this case: _____

_____

_____

_____

_____

Exercise 2.6

Work in small groups (three or four students). Discuss your answers to exercise 2.5.

Language Review

Read the key word or phrase (in bold) in the left column. Circle the letter of the choice that is related to the key word or phrase.

1. **split**   a. help   b. divide   c. decorate

2. **annual**   a. once a day   b. once a month   c. once a year

3. **slogan**   a. advertisement   b. legal problems   c. drinking item

4. **approximately**   a. most of the time   b. the same amount   c. more or less

5. **range**   a. vary   b. look at carefully   c. suggest

6. **amicably**   a. like friends   b. like thieves   c. like children

7. **cap**   a. on the bottom   b. in the bottle   c. on the top

8. **contest**   a. answer   b. competition   c. kind of drink

9. **regarding**   a. under   b. in order to   c. about

10. **involve**   a. include   b. explain   c. omit

11. **purchase**   a. understand   b. buy   c. travel

12. **resolve**   a. find a solution to b. smile at someone   c. eat too much

13. **come up with**   a. produce   b. control   c. justify

14. **testify**   a. in a courtroom   b. in a restaurant   c. in a factory

Be sure to visit <www.press.umich.edu/esl> for ideas on related Web sites, videos, and other activities.

UNIT 3

Cell Phones

INTRODUCTION

Ten years ago, cell phones were not so common. Now they are everywhere. At first, there was some controversy about a possible connection between brain cancer and cell phone use. However, that has given way to concern that cell phones are a public nuisance and possibly a traffic danger.

Exercise 3.1

Complete the questions in this survey.

1. Have you ever spoken on a cell phone?

   _____ yes   _____ no

2. Do you own a cell phone?

   _____ yes   _____ no

3. Have you ever received a cell phone call in a public place?

    _____ yes   _____ no

4. Have you ever received a cell phone call in a public place where the phone call was a disturbance, such as in class or at a movie?

    _____ yes   _____ no

    If yes, describe the situation. (If it has happened many times, describe what you consider to be the worst situation.)

    _____

    _____

    _____

    _____

    _____

    _____

    _____

    If no, describe a situation in which someone near you received a cell phone call in a setting where the phone call was a disturbance.

    _____

    _____

    _____

    _____

    _____

5. Do you think that people who receive cell phone calls in certain public places such as movie theaters or classrooms should have to pay a fine? Why or why not?

    _____

    _____

_____

_____

_____

6. Do you think people should be able to use cell phones when they are driving? _____

   Why or why not?

_____

_____

_____

_____

_____

_____

_____

Exercise 3.2

Work in small groups to discuss your answers to exercise 3.1. Do the members of your group think that cell phones are a problem in any way?

Exercise 3.3

Read this short piece about cell phone usage on Japanese trains.

In Japan, many people commute to work by train. In fact, many of these people spend very large amounts of time commuting each week, and many of them sleep on the train to and from work. Because cell phones that are ringing and people who are talking on them are a disturbance, some train lines have banned the use of cell phones inside the train cars. Calls must be made from the passageways between the train cars. In essence, cell phones have been banned from the primary method of travel in Japan.

Exercise 3.4

Do you agree with this ban on cell phone use in some Japanese train cars? Why or why not?

_____

_____

_____

_____

_____

Exercise 3.5

Now work in small groups to discuss your answers to the main question in exercise 3.4.

Exercise 3.6

Read this information about driving a vehicle while using a cell phone and then answer the questions regarding this topic.

There is evidence that drivers using cell phones have had accidents because they were using their cell phones. In some cases, the drivers have been killed; in others, innocent bystanders or other drivers and passengers have been killed. Because of these data, some countries (and some states in the United States) have banned talking on cell phones while driving. For example, the use of cell phones while a vehicle is in motion has been banned in Australia, Brazil, Chile, Great Britain, Israel, Italy, Japan, Portugal, Singapore, Sweden, and Taiwan. In the month after cell phone use by drivers was banned in Sweden, the number of accidents caused by drivers using their cell phones fell by 75 percent.

Question: These statistics are impressive, but vehicle accidents are caused by many factors. In your opinion, should drivers be prohibited from talking on their cell phones while driving?

_____

_____

_____

_____

_____

_____

Exercise 3.7

Work in small groups (three or four students). Discuss your answers to the question in exercise 3.6. What is the consensus of your group? Should the use of cell phones by drivers be banned?

Exercise 3.8

Read this true story about a car crash involving a driver who was using a cell phone.

> Patricia Pena, age 27, and her husband had worked and waited and saved for seven years to have their first child, Morgan Lee. When the family's finances were stable, Patricia was able to resign from her job to be a full-time stay-at-home mom. Unfortunately, only three days later an unimaginable tragedy occurred.
>
> On November 3, 1999, Patricia Pena was driving home with her two-and-a-half-year-old daughter, Morgan Lee. She and Morgan had gone to visit Patricia's sister and her son Christian, who was four years old. Morgan loved playing with Christian.
>
> It was almost Morgan's usual nap time, and Patricia had to choose between letting Morgan go to gym class with Christian or taking her home for her nap. Patricia decided to take Morgan home for her nap.

Two minutes later on the drive home, a man ran a stop sign while traveling at 45 miles per hour and hit Patricia's car broadside. The impact killed Morgan as she sat in her car seat. Patricia found herself staring at her baby, who was bleeding from her head. Morgan was not breathing, but she was still alive. Morgan was taken to the hospital. However, she died shortly after. Patricia was there when her daughter died.

The driver of the car was not concentrating on the road or his vehicle. He was talking on his cell phone when he ran the stop sign and crashed into the car that Patricia and Morgan were in.

Exercise 3.9

If you were a judge who had to decide consequences for the driver who caused this crash, what punishment, if any, would you give him? Three facts that may be important here are

1. the driver did not intend to kill anyone,
2. the driver was not focusing 100 percent on driving the vehicle, and
3. the driver actually killed an innocent person.

Write your recommended punishment and reasons for making this particular recommendation.

_____

_____

_____

_____

_____

_____

_____

_____

_____

Exercise 3.10

Work in small groups of three to five members. Take turns explaining what punishment you recommended. Be sure to offer reasons for your decision. Speakers
should be prepared to answer questions from the other group members.
What is the consensus of your group?

_____

_____

_____

_____

_____

_____

Exercise 3.11

Now turn to communication activity 52 to find out what happened to the driver
whose lack of attention caused a young child's death.

 Language Review

These questions contain underlined words that are key vocabulary words that
you should remember. Write a synonym or definition for the vocabulary words
and then provide a logical answer to the questions.

1. If the police arrest you for drinking and then driving a car, this might result
   in the <u>suspension</u> of what?

   suspension   _____

   answer: _____

2. When was the last time that you were <u>outraged</u>?

   outraged   _____

   answer: _____

3. If you want to sell your car, what is the best way to <u>get the word out</u>?

   get the word out _____

   answer: _____

4. Do you think the driver in the case in this unit is guilty of <u>negligence</u>?

   negligence _____

   answer: _____

5. What is a major <u>nuisance</u> at picnics?

   nuisance _____

   answer: _____

6. How much is the usual <u>fine</u> for speeding?

   fine _____

   answer: _____

7. Would it be a <u>tragedy</u> to lose your umbrella?

   tragedy _____

   answer: _____

8. Do you think that drinking alcohol is <u>in essence</u> the same as taking drugs?

   in essence _____

   answer: _____

9. Did you ever <u>threaten</u> to quit your job?

   threaten _____

   answer: _____

10. When did the <u>ban</u> on smoking in public buildings go into effect?

    ban _____

    answer: _____

11. Do you think that there is any real <u>evidence</u> that beings from outer space have visited our planet?

   evidence _____

   answer: _____

12. Have you seen any <u>data</u> that would lead you to believe that smoking causes lung cancer?

   data _____

   answer: _____

13. How often do you take a <u>nap</u> in the afternoon?

   nap _____

   answer: _____

14. What foods does your diet <u>lack</u> that you would like to add?

   lack _____

   answer: _____

15. Have you ever <u>run</u> a stop sign?

   run _____

   answer: _____

Be sure to visit <www.press.umich.edu/esl> for ideas on related Web sites, videos, and other activities.

An Interviewer's Ideal Person to Interview

INTRODUCTION

Who are the people who have shaped the destiny of our world the most? If you could interview any person—living or dead—who would be your choice?

Exercise 4.1

You are an interviewer for a major TV network. If you could get to interview any three people, living or dead, from the following group of people, who would you interview, why would you choose that person, and what would you ask him or her? Write your answers below.

Margaret Thatcher	Tina Turner	Martin Luther King, Jr.	Elton John
Sadam Hussein	Nelson Mandela	Bill Gates	the Dalai Lama
Barbra Streisand	Eva Peron	Maradona	John Lennon
Pelé	Elvis Presley	Emperor Hirohito	Monica Seles
Stephen King	Abraham Lincoln	John F. Kennedy	Columbus
Mohandas Gandhi	Albert Einstein	Jimmy Carter	Amelia Earhart
Madonna	Abigail Van Buren	Thomas Edison	Lucille Ball
Anwar Sadat	Gloria Steinem	Princess Diana	William Shakespeare
Richard Nixon	Golda Meir	Socrates	Winston Churchill
Fidel Castro	Mao Tse-Tung	the Pope	Walt Disney
Charlie Chaplin	Bette Davis	Cesar Chávez	Eleanor Roosevelt
Magic Johnson	Simon Bolívar	Steven Spielberg	Michael Jackson
Mother Teresa	Jonas Salk	Neil Armstrong	Mikhail Gorbachev
Tiger Woods	Bill Clinton	Hillary Clinton	

a. person: _____

   reasons: _____

   _____

   _____

   questions: _____

   _____

   _____

b. person: _____

   reasons: _____

   _____

   _____

   questions: _____

   _____

   _____

c. person: _____

   reasons: _____

   _____

   _____

   questions: _____

   _____

   _____

Exercise 4.2

Work in groups of five or six students. One student will act as the group leader to make sure that things go smoothly. This student will call on group members to make their presentations. Another student will act as timekeeper. Students will have no more than 60 seconds to tell the name of one person that they want to interview, the reasons for choosing that person, and perhaps one question that they would like to ask that person. After all of the group members have presented one of their choices, repeat the process again. It is important to stick to the time limit in this activity to make sure that all students get to participate in this speaking practice.

Exercise 4.3

Role Play

Prepare a list of five questions that you would like to ask your famous person. Then work in groups of three students. One person is the famous person who has to answer all of the interviewer's questions. One person is the reporter who will ask the questions. The third person is a recorder. This person should listen to the interview and write a small report of what was said during the interview. The third person can ask questions if he or she does not understand something. Take turns playing these roles.

Exercise 4.4

More Role Play

The speaking practice in exercise 4.3 is a little difficult. Therefore, it is important to do this practice one more time. Repeat the exercise 4.3 activity but with two different students. Try to take a different role this time (i.e., if you were the reporter last time, if at all possible you should be the famous person or the recorder this time).

Exercise 4.5

Think of one other person who you would like to interview that is not on the list for this unit. Who is this person? Why would you like to interview this person? What question(s) would you ask?

person: _____

reasons: _____

_____

_____

_____

_____

questions: _____

_____

_____

_____

_____

Exercise 4.6

Work in pairs or small groups. Take turns presenting the name of the additional person that you would like to interview, your reasons for choosing this person, and the questions that you would ask that person. If you do not understand something that the presenter says, make sure that you ask that student to clarify the information.

Language Review

Read the key word or phrase (in bold) in the left column. Circle the letter of the choice that is related to the key word or phrase.

1. **clarify**   a. make something clear   b. make something unclear

2. **interview**   a. ask someone questions   b. look between two things

3. **call on**   a. a teacher calls on students   b. a waiter calls on customers

4. **participate in**   a. take part of something   b. take part in something

5. **make sure**   a. verify that it is so   b. remember that it is so

6. **go smoothly**   a. have bad results   b. have good results

7. **as well**   a. excellent; great   b. and; including

8. **role**   a. character in a movie   b. turn over quickly
                             or another drama

9. **act as**   a. work very hard in   b. take the role of

10. **stick to a plan**   a. create a plan   b. follow a plan

11. **get to**   a. have an opportunity to   b. intend to; make a plan to

12. **shape**   a. form; create   b. take quickly; seize

Be sure to visit <www.press.umich.edu/esl> for ideas on related Web sites, videos, and other activities.

Jokes: Is It Funny?
Culture and Humor

antlers

INTRODUCTION

This unit involves humor. What is funny? What is not funny? What works as a joke can vary tremendously from culture to culture and certainly from language to language.

Exercise 5.1

Read these two jokes. What are your reactions to these two jokes? Answer the questions about the jokes.

JOKE 1

Two novice hunters were dragging a deer back to their truck. Another hunter walked by and said, "I don't want to tell you what to do, but it's easier if you drag the deer in the other direction so the antlers don't dig into the ground."

After the third hunter left, the two decided to try it his way. After a while, one said to the other, "Man, that guy was totally right. This is easier."

"Yeah," the other replied, "but we keep getting farther and farther away from the truck."

JOKE 2

One day two guys were driving to the store. They came to a busy inter-section. The light was red, but the driver drove through without stopping. The passenger was shocked. "What are you doing?"

The driver replied, "Hey, it's OK. My mother always drives like this. Don't worry."

A few minutes later they came to another traffic light, and it was red. The driver didn't even slow down. He just ran the light. The passenger was terrified. "Are you nuts? Stop driving like this!" The driver replied, "Hey, it's OK. My mother always drives like this."

Just a few minutes later, they came to another traffic light at a busy intersection, but this time the light was green. The driver did not go through the light. He hit the brakes as hard as he could to stop the car.

The passenger was furious. "This is the third time you almost got us killed. Why did you stop at a green light?"

The driver replied, "Well, my mother might be coming the other way."

1. Is Joke 1 funny to you? How would you rate it using the four choices below?

_____ very funny

_____ a little funny

_____ not very funny

_____ not funny at all

2. Why do you think this joke is (or is not) funny to you?

_____

_____

_____

_____

_____

_____

3. Is Joke 2 funny to you? How would you rate it using the four choices below?

_____ very funny

_____ a little funny

_____ not very funny

_____ not funny at all

4. Why do you think this joke is (or is not) funny to you?

_____

_____

_____

_____

_____

5. Can you think of anything that could be changed in either of the jokes to make them funny (or more funny) to you?

_____

_____

_____

_____

_____

Exercise 5.2

Work in small groups. Discuss your answers to exercise 5.1. Which of the jokes is thought to be funnier, 1 or 2? What reasons do the members of your discussion group give for their opinion?

Exercise 5.3

Read these four jokes. Rank them from 1 to 4, with 1 being the funniest and 4 being the least funny.

___ THE MISUSED LAUNDRY DETERGENT

A little boy went to the grocery story and bought a huge box of laundry detergent. The grocer asked if the boy was going to help his parents with the dirty laundry. The boy replied, "Oh, no. I am going to wash my dog." The man tried to explain to the boy that the detergent might kill the dog, but the boy was sure about what he was doing. Two weeks later, the little boy came into the store, and the grocer asked, "Hey, how's your dog?" The little boy got a sad look on his face and said, "Oh, he died two weeks ago." The grocer felt bad and couldn't help saying, "Gosh, I tried to warn you that the detergent was dangerous." The little boy shook his head and said, "The detergent didn't kill him." The grocer was confused and said, "Oh, really? Then what did?" The little boy said, "I think it was the spin cycle."

___ THE STOLEN STEAK

One day a butcher was going out of his shop. When he opened the door, a dog ran in and jumped up on the meat counter. The dog grabbed an expensive steak and ran out the door. The butcher was really angry, but he knew the owner of the dog. He was a lawyer who lived a few houses away from the butcher shop. The butcher immediately called the bad dog's owner. The butcher introduced himself and asked, "I have a legal question for you. If your dog stole an expensive steak from my shop, would you be legally responsible for paying for the steak?" The lawyer thought for a very short time and answered, "Why, yes, of course I would have to pay you. How much was the steak?" "$10," replied the butcher. The next day the butcher received an envelope from the lawyer. When he opened it, he found a check for $10. He also found a note that read "Please send your payment of $125 for legal services."

___ PROBLEMS IN THE GARDEN OF EDEN

Eve lived alone in the Garden of Eden. One day she shouted out, "God, I love this beautiful garden and that snake, but I'm not so happy." "What's wrong?" asked God. Eve replied, "Well, I can't think of anything new to talk about to the snake, and I'm so tired of eating apples every day." God said, "I have the solution. I will give you a man." Eve didn't know what a man was, so she asked God to explain. God said, "A man is a creature with many bad traits. He will lie, and he will make your life difficult, but he will hunt and provide for you. He will do childish things, and he can't think very well, so he'll need your advice to make important decisions." Eve thought about this a bit and said, "OK, this creature called a man sounds good. Give me one. But what is the catch?" God answered, "Well, there is one condition, Eve. He will be a bit arrogant and self-centered, so you have to let him believe that I made him first, OK? Just remember that it's our little secret . . . you know, woman to woman."

___ A NECESSARY LOAN

One day a woman walked into a big bank in the middle of downtown Chicago. She asked to speak to the loan officer. She said, "I'm going to Europe on business, and I need to borrow $10,000." The loan officer replied, "Well, for a loan of that amount, we'll need something substantial as collateral." Without hesitating, the woman handed the loan officer the keys to her new Rolls Royce, which was parked in front of the bank. The loan officer knew that the woman's Rolls Royce was worth at least $200,000, so he approved the loan. The bank president and other officials had a good laugh at this silly person for using a $200,000 car as collateral for a $10,000 loan. To keep the car safe, the bank people parked the car in a safe corner of the bank's private underground parking lot. Two weeks later, the woman returned from her trip to Europe and gave the loan officer the $10,000 plus the interest, which was only $32.68. The loan officer said, "Excuse me for asking this, but I have to know. We were happy to have your loan business here. We checked out your credit. You are a multimillionaire. Why did you bother to borrow $10,000 from us?" The woman replied, "Where else could I park my car so safely in Chicago for two weeks for $32.68?"

Exercise 5.4

Which of the four jokes in exercise 5.3 did you think was the funniest? Why?

_____

_____

_____

_____

_____

_____

_____

Exercise 5.5

Work in small groups of four to six people. One person should be the group leader. The group leader should first ask each person's rankings for the four jokes in Exercise 5.3. Total up the rankings to find out which joke was the funniest according to the members of your group. Then each person should tell which joke he or she thought was the funniest and then tell the reasons for choosing this joke. (Use the answers from exercise 5.4.)

What was your group's consensus for the funniest joke?

_____ The Misused Laundry Detergent

_____ The Stolen Steak

_____ Problems in the Garden of Eden

_____ A Necessary Loan

Exercise 5.6

Can you think of a joke in your native language or another language you know? Write out the joke in English. Then take turns sharing your joke with the rest of the class. Do not use jokes with foul language or inappropriate content.

_____

_____

_____

_____

_____

_____

_____

_____

Exercise 5.7

Ask a native speaker to tell you a joke. (You could also consult a magazine, a book, or the Internet if you cannot talk to a native speaker.) Write down the joke here.

_____

_____

_____

_____

_____

_____

_____

_____

Exercise 5.8

Before class, practice telling the joke from exercise 5.7 in English. You can use your book or notes if you want, but you should not have to read the joke. Try to memorize the joke. Then get into groups of four to six members. Take turns telling your jokes.

 Language Review

Read the key word or phrase (in bold) in the left column. Circle the letter of the choice that is related to the key word or phrase.

1. **huge**   a. large   b. tiny

2. **hesitate**   a. wait   b. proceed

3. **spin**   a. move in a line   b. move in a circle

4. **drag**   a. pull   b. drive

5. **antlers**   a. an animal's horns   b. an animal's feet

6. **rationale**   a. results   b. reasons

7. **laundry**   a. washing clothes   b. buying clothes

8. **traits**   a. attempts   b. characteristics

9. **the catch**   a. negative part of an offer b. positive part of an offer

10. **arrogant**   a. too much confidence   b. too much sadness

11. **detergent**   a. kind of water   b. kind of soap

12. **try it his way** a. go to someone's house   b. take someone's advice

13. **totally**   a. mostly   b. completely

14. **butcher**   a. sells vegetables   b. sells meat

15. **grab**   a. take   b. provide

16. **reply**   a. play again   b. answer

17. **nuts**   a. sad   b. crazy

18. **furious**   a. angry   b. interested

19. **legal**   a. law   b. feelings

20. **solution**   a. answer to a problem   b. cause of a problem

21. **consult** (a book) a. check in a book   b. pay for a book

22. **substantial**   a. rather small   b. rather large

23. **check out**   a. investigate   b. produce

24. **inappropriate**   a. not correct; not suitable   b. not mine; not yours

25. **self-centered**   a. thinking of others too much   b. thinking of oneself too much

Be sure to visit <www.press.umich.edu/esl> for ideas on related Web sites, videos, and other activities.

UNIT 6

Proverbs

INTRODUCTION

Proverb: "Birds of a feather flock together." What do you think this sentence means? A proverb is a brief saying that teaches a lesson. The proverb above means that people most often spend time with people who are similar to them. For example, if Sandra likes to bake and Mindy likes to cook, people might say, "Birds of a feather flock together!" This means they have something in common. Proverbs are interesting because they reveal things about cultures and values.

Exercise 6.1

Read these eight proverbs. Try to guess the meaning of each proverb. Write your guesses on the lines.

a. Actions speak louder than words.

_____

_____

b. All's well that ends well.

_____

_____

c. Out of the frying pan and into the fire.

_____

_____

d. An idle mind is the devil's workshop.

_____

_____

e. Don't burn bridges behind you.

_____

_____

f. You scratch my back, and I'll scratch yours.

_____

_____

g. Don't close one door until you have opened another.

_____

_____

h. Blood is thicker than water.

_____

_____

Exercise 6.2

Now work in groups of four students. One student should do a and b, another c and d, another e and f, and the other g and h. Take turns discussing what you think the meanings of these proverbs are. Give reasons for what you have written as your guesses.

Exercise 6.3

Continue working in groups of four members. After you finish exercises 6.1 and 6.2, check your answers using the following communication activities. Each student in the group will be responsible for reading the answer with the correct meaning of two proverbs.

Student 1 should read communication activity 14, student 2 can read communication activity 27, student 3 can read communication activity 45, and student 4 can read communication activity 60.

Take turns explaining in your own words what the correct meanings of these proverbs are. Do not just read the words from the back of the book. Try to use your own words as much as possible.

Exercise 6.4

Write a situation that explains one of the proverbs in this lesson. Write the proverb on the line after the situation.

Situation

_____

_____

_____

_____

_____

_____

Proverb

_____

_____

Exercise 6.5

Work in small groups (three students is the best group size). Take turns reading your situation from exercise 6.4 aloud (or telling your situation if you can remember all the details). After a person has told his or her situation, the others should try to guess what the proverb is.

Exercise 6.6

Write down a proverb in your native language or another language you know. Translate the words (literal translation) and see if anyone from a different language background can guess the meaning of the proverb. Then work with a native speaker to see if you can find an English proverb that has a similar meaning. (Sometimes the translations will be very similar, but sometimes they will be very different.)

In another language

_____

Literal translation

_____

Equivalent English proverb

_____

 Language Review

Use the vocabulary items in the box to complete the sentences.

feather	flock	brief	as long as	scratch

1. We wrote a _____ letter to the company to explain our situation.

2. _____ you take this medicine, you will be fine.

3. A _____ of seagulls crowded around the people on the beach.

4. The doctor told me not to _____ the cut area on my arm, but it itches.

5. We found a red _____ near the car door, so we believe there is a red cardinal that comes to our backyard.

Be sure to visit <www.press.umich.edu/esl> for ideas on related Web sites, videos, and other activities.

Put the Story Together:
The Patient

INTRODUCTION

One thing that most people dread is a trip to see their doctor. For whatever reason, this trip seems to bring out the worst in most of us. This unit deals with a rather unique medical problem.

Exercise 7.1

Work in groups of eight.* Each student will have a piece of a story. Try to put the story together.

---

*If there are extra students, these students should be judges. The judges should listen to the story lines and decide if the eight students have put themselves in the correct order or not. Conversely, if there are not eight students, the teacher should participate, and perhaps one or two of the lines could be copied on a sheet of paper that could be placed on the floor in the correct position within the story. (See step 4.)

Step 1. Each student should look at one of these communication activities: 2, 9, 20, 29, 40, 53, 72, and 88.

Step 2. Write your activity number in the box and write your sentence on the line.

☐ _____

Step 3. You have one minute to read and memorize your piece of the story. You do not have to use the exact same words, but you do need to express the same idea.

Step 4. The eight students should stand up and try to put themselves (their pieces of the story) in order by taking turns saying (not reading) their lines aloud.

Exercise 7.2

Work in small groups. Write another strip story like the one in exercise 7.1. Try to have a funny or surprising ending.

 Language Review

Match the definition in the right column with the correct word in the left column.

Vocabulary

____ 1. really

____ 2. complained

____ 3. press

____ 4. suffer

____ 5. stumped

____ 6. specialist

Definition

a. unable to find an answer

b. put steady force on something

c. very much

d. a person who focuses on one particular area of study

e. experience pain

f. expressed unhappiness or displeasure

 Be sure to visit <www.press.umich.edu/esl> for ideas on related Web sites, videos, and other activities.

UNIT 8

Life after Death?

In Woody Allen's *Sleeper* (1973), a nerdish store owner is revived out of cryostasis into a future world. (Courtesy of the Film Stills Archive of the Museum of Modern Art, New York.)

INTRODUCTION

One question has kept human beings busy since the dawn of time: What happens to us when we cease to breathe air on this planet? Do we go to another place? Are we born again as another being? Do we just go away? This unit seeks to examine our beliefs on this topic.

Exercise 8.1

Here are some statements that are connected to the question of what happens to us when we die. Circle 1 if you *strongly agree* with the statement, 2 if you *agree* with the statement, 3 if you are *not sure* of your opinion regarding the statement, 4 if you *disagree* with the statement, and 5 if you *strongly disagree* with the statement.

a. 1 2 3 4 5   Human beings continue to exist in some form after we die.

_____

_____

_____

b. 1 2 3 4 5   Our fate after death is decided by God.

_____

_____

_____

c. 1 2 3 4 5   Good people go to a different place than bad people do.

_____

_____

_____

d. 1 2 3 4 5   Some people choose to be frozen immediately after death with the hope that one day scientists will have discovered a cure for the disease from which they died. Cryonics is the science that offers this technology. If I had the money and possibility to do this, I would do this.

_____

_____

_____

e. 1 2 3 4 5   What happens to us after death is connected to our actions toward our fellow human beings while we are alive on Earth.

_____

_____

_____

f. 1 2 3 4 5   I prefer to be cremated when I die rather than be buried.

_____

_____

_____

g. 1 2 3 4 5   When I die, I will be able to see relatives and friends who have already died.

_____

_____

_____

h. 1 2 3 4 5   I believe in the concepts of heaven and hell.

_____

_____

_____

i. 1 2 3 4 5   When we die, that's it. Our body turns into dust, and our brain, body, and soul no longer exist.

_____

_____

_____

j. 1 2 3 4 5   At some point after death, humans come back to Earth as another living creature.

_____

_____

_____

Exercise 8.2

Work in groups to discuss your answers to exercise 8.1.

For which two statements do your group members have the widest variation in answers? ___ and ___ . Which statement proved to be the most controversial? ___ . Why was this the most controversial issue?

_____

_____

_____

_____

_____

_____

_____

_____

Exercise 8.3

The science of cryonics has attracted attention for many years. It is technology that provides people the opportunity to be frozen immediately after their death and then defrosted when a cure has been found for whatever disease killed them. People have the opportunity to freeze their entire bodies, to freeze their heads only (to be cloned onto another body later), and to take their pets with them.

a. If you could, would you have yourself frozen after death? Why or why not?

_____

_____

_____

_____

_____

_____

b. Let us imagine for one minute that this technology works and that we are
    indeed able to be revived later in the future. What are some of the negative
    aspects of waking up possibly 100 years after you "went to sleep"?

_____

_____

_____

_____

_____

_____

_____

_____

_____

_____

c. Do you think this technology will ever become reality? Why or why not?

_____

_____

_____

_____

_____

_____

_____

_____

d. Some people object to this technology because they believe it is an example of science trying to take the place of God. Do you agree or disagree with the idea that this technology is an example of human beings trying to go too far?

_____

_____

_____

_____

_____

_____

_____

_____

Exercise 8.4

Work in small groups to discuss your answers to the questions and issues in exercise 8.3.

 Language Review

Read the key word or phrase (in bold) in the left column. Circle the letter of the choice that is related to the key word or phrase.

1. **dawn**   a. beginning   b. end

2. **cease**   a. begin   b. end

3. **breathe**   a. lungs   b. ankles

4. **seek**   a. look for   b. get away

5. **fate**   a. destiny   b. origin

6. **cremate**   a. make into a liquid   b. make into ashes

7. **rather than**   a. in addition to   b. instead of

8. **bury**   a. put in a machine   b. put in the ground

9. **relatives**   a. family members   b. close friends

10. **concept**   a. starting point   b. idea

11. **A turns into B.**   a. Now we have only A.   b. Now we have only B.

12. **dust**   a. powder   b. air

13. **creature**   a. dead thing   b. living thing

14. **variation**   a. similarity   b. difference

15. **controversial**   a. Many people agree.   b. Many people disagree.

16. **defrost**   a. become unfrozen   b. become frozen

17. **cure**   a. cause a disease   b. stop a disease

18. **clone**   a. original   b. copy

19. **aspects**   a. features; parts   b. desires; wishes

20. **object to**   a. be a good thing   b. disagree with

Be sure to visit <www.press.umich.edu/esl> for ideas on related Web sites, videos, and other activities.

Finish the Story:
The Young Boy's Dilemma

INTRODUCTION

Can you guess what happened? The clues in the story will help you figure out the ending of the story.

Exercise 9.1

Read the following true story.

Joshua Bernardo is a seven-year-old boy who lives in Vacaville, California. One day, when he was walking through his house, something unexpected happened. This occurrence was such a surprise that it left Joshua unable to walk. Several hours later, specialists arrived and helped Joshua with his dilemma.

Exercise 9.2

Work in small groups. Come up with three possible answers for this question: What was the occurrence that left Joshua unable to walk? Write your three answers in the spaces below. Circle the number of the most likely explanation.

1. _____

2. _____

3. _____

Exercise 9.3

Each group should choose the best answer from exercise 9.2 and tell it to the class. Which answer is the most plausible? Be ready to give reasons to back up your answer. When another group presents their answers, ask questions to clarify any doubts that you might have or give reasons to show why their answers are not likely to be correct.

Exercise 9.4

Guessing Game

Step 1. A panel of experts should be chosen (perhaps one person per group). The panel should sit in a row of chairs at the front of the room.
Step 2. Only the panel members should read communication activity 56 on page 150 to find out the young boy's problem.
Step 3. The other students should divide into teams and take turns asking questions about the situation.
Step 4. The panel of experts should give answers (and hints if needed) until one of the teams can guess what really happened to the young boy.

Language Review

Match the definition in the right column with the correct word or phrase in the left column.

Vocabulary
Definition

___ 1. spilled   a. unable to move from somewhere

___ 2. piggy bank   b. poured or dropped something by mistake

___ 3. stepped in   c. made less tight

___ 4. barefoot   d. container, shaped like an animal, where children
          keep money

___ 5. stuck

      e. put one's foot in
___ 6. loosened

      f. without shoes or socks
___ 7. occurrence

      g. support
___ 8. back up

      h. serious problem
___ 9. row

      i. event; happening
___ 10. dilemma

      j. line

Be sure to visit <www.press.umich.edu/esl> for ideas on related Web sites, videos, and other activities.

UNIT 10

The Death Penalty

INTRODUCTION

Only a handful of countries around the world punish murderers by executing them. The United States is one of these few countries that have capital punishment. It is indeed a controversial issue.

Exercise 10.1

Read the following proverbs and try to guess what each one means. Then try to decide what value is being taught. Write your guesses on the lines that follow.

a. One good turn deserves another.

_____

_____

_____

_____

_____

_____

b. An eye for an eye, a tooth for a tooth.

_____

_____

_____

_____

_____

c. You made your bed, now lie in it.

_____

_____

_____

_____

_____

d. Turn the other cheek.

_____

_____

_____

_____

_____

_____

Exercise 10.2

Work in small groups. Discuss your responses to the proverbs in exercise 10.1. When you have finished, look at communication activity 39 to find out what these proverbs mean.

Exercise 10.3

The proverbs in exercise 10.1 refer to personal responsibility and how people respond to being mistreated by others. Do you have any proverbs or expressions in your language that talk about this topic? Write down an appropriate proverb and its translation.

In another language

_____

_____

Literal translation

_____

_____

Equivalent English proverb

_____

_____

Exercise 10.4

Work in small groups and discuss the value taught in the proverb you wrote in exercise 10.3. Do you think this proverb illustrates a value that is generally accepted by the mainstream population in your culture, or do you think most people disagree with it?

Exercise 10.5

How much do you know about the death penalty in the United States? Take this quiz and find out. Write *T* if you think the statement is true and write *F* if you think the statement is false.

____ 1. The death penalty saves taxpayers money because it is cheaper to execute someone than to keep that person in prison for the rest of his or her life.

____ 2. Since the death penalty was reinstated in 1976, more black people have been executed than white people.

____ 3. In most states with the death penalty, you could be executed even if you suffer from mental retardation.

____ 4. If you commit a crime in certain states like Massachusetts or Wisconsin, you cannot receive the death penalty.

____ 5. Hanging has not been used as a method of execution in the United States for over 30 years.

____ 6. No woman has been executed in the United States for more than 25 years.

____ 7. The Supreme Court has said that defendants who were 16 or 17 years old at the time of their crime can receive the death penalty.

Exercise 10.6

Compare answers with a partner. Then check your answers in communication activity 75. Were you surprised by the answers? Would these answers be the same or similar in your country? What would be different? Why do you think this is so?

Exercise 10.7

Thirty-eight states in the United States utilize the death penalty as a form of punishment for convicted criminals. Do you agree with the practice of capital punishment, the sentence of death for a criminal convicted of a very serious crime? _____

Why or why not?

_____

_____

_____

_____

_____

_____

_____

What—if any—crime is serious enough to be punished by death?

_____

_____

_____

_____

_____

In your opinion, what is an appropriate punishment for murder, the unlawful killing of a person?

_____

_____

_____

_____

_____

_____

_____

In your opinion, what is an appropriate punishment for rape, the crime of forcing another person to have sex?

_____

_____

_____

_____

_____

_____

If you disagree with capital punishment, what would you do if someone killed a member of your family?

_____

_____

_____

_____

_____

If you agree with the death penalty, would you be willing to administer the punishment? _____ Give reasons for your answer.

_____

_____

_____

_____

Exercise 10.8

In the United States, there are currently three forms of capital punishment that are commonly used—electrocution, the gas chamber, and lethal injection. Read the descriptions and possible drawbacks of each and answer the questions that follow.

Death by Electrocution

Two thousand volts of electricity are sent through the body for three minutes. Electrodes are attached to the legs and to the head by use of a wet sponge and a metal skullcap.

Dr. Harold Hillman, a British expert on execution, suggests that the bodily fluids reach the boiling point, which is why witnesses often see steam coming from the person. He believes that electrocution is extremely painful and that there is no reason to believe the person loses consciousness while being electrocuted.

Death by Lethal Injection

The person is strapped down and given a deadly dose of barbiturates intravenously. According to Hugo Bedau, professor of philosophy at Tufts University, ". . . it can take some time for technicians to find a proper vein for the injection . . . and . . . needles have also been known to fly out in the middle of the injection."

Death by Gas

The prisoner is strapped into a chair, and cyanide gas is administered through a hole in the floor. Death takes from three to four minutes.

According to JoAnn Bren Guernsey, some experts say that prisoners have been known to go into convulsions or choke to death on the gas.

Does the form of punishment affect your opinion of the death penalty? _____

Would you be more likely to support the death penalty if you could choose which of the current methods were used? Why or why not?

_____

_____

_____

_____

_____

Opponents of the death penalty argue that it is inhumane—cruel and unusual punishment, which is specifically prohibited by the U.S. Constitution. Do you agree with this statement? _____

Do you think a person guilty of murder has the right to expect humane treatment? Give reasons for your answer.

_____

_____

_____

_____

_____

Exercise 10.9

Work in small groups. Discuss your answers to the questions in exercise 10.8.

Exercise 10.10

A common argument against the use of the death penalty is that killing a person is against the will of God. Consider these excerpts from the Bible.

> "Whoever strikes a man so that he dies shall be put to death" (Exodus 21:12). "Whosoever sheds a man's blood, by man shall his blood be shed" (Genesis 9:6).

What is your response to these statements?

_____

_____

_____

_____

_____

_____

_____

_____

Exercise 10.11

In the United States, 38 states have legalized capital punishment, 11 have not legalized capital punishment, and 1 state stands alone in its position on capital punishment. Read this excerpt from an article about the governor of Illinois and his reservations about capital punishment.

Republican governor George Ryan of Illinois has serious concerns about his state's use of the death penalty for serious criminals. Since 1987, 13 inmates have been released from Illinois prisons because of problems with the criminal justice system. In most of the cases, inmates were released because of new DNA evidence, new witnesses, unqualified defense attorneys, or confessions from others.

Governor Ryan's position is that "There is no margin for error when it comes to putting a person to death. Until [he] can be sure that everyone sentenced to death in Illinois is truly guilty—until [he] can be sure with moral certainty that no innocent man or woman is facing a lethal injection—no one will meet that fate."

On January 31, 2000, Governor Ryan did something that no other state had done. Although Governor Ryan supports the use of the death penalty, he put on hold all executions scheduled in the state of Illinois until further examination of the criminal justice system could take place.

Exercise 10.12

Do you agree with Governor Ryan's decision to put all executions on hold?

_____

Give reasons for your answer.

_____

_____

_____

_____

_____

_____

_____

What message does this send to the families of the people who have been executed in Illinois?

_____

_____

_____

_____

_____

_____

Exercise 10.13

Read this summary of a situation that arose when a well-known clothing company published some controversial advertisements.

> In January 2000, Italian clothing company Benetton's advertisements featuring 26 death row inmates sparked controversy and angered the families of the inmates' victims as well as victims' rights advocates. The ads, which appeared in magazines and on billboards, featured photos of the inmates, along with interviews with them about sports, politics, their childhoods, and their experiences in prison. Victims' families have protested the ads, saying they are a painful reminder of their losses. Others have criticized the company for using convicted murderers to sell clothing. Benetton officials have defended the campaign, saying it was intended to "promote discussion and communication" about the death penalty debate.

What is your opinion of the Benetton ads? Should the company have the right to advertise in any way it sees fit? Give reasons for your answer.

_____

_____

_____

_____

_____

_____

_____

Exercise 10.14

Role Play

Scene: In a closed courtroom, several people are given the opportunity to voice their opinions about capital punishment. Possible participants: a man convicted of murdering a woman, the man's wife, one of the man's children, the victim's husband, one of the victim's children, the executioner, a priest or another spiritual adviser.

Work in groups of four to six members. Each person should take one of the roles. Be sure that no two people in the same group have the same role.

Your role:

_____

Your position on this issue:

_____

_____

_____

_____

_____

_____

_____

_____

_____

_____

_____

_____

Language Review

Use the vocabulary items in the box to complete the sentences.

confession	capital punishment	convicted	appropriate
administer	currently	drawbacks	consciousness
lethal	intravenously	convulsions	unlawful
values	inhumanely	inmate	victim

1. People who disagree with the death penalty don't want a _____

   person to be treated _____; they want the

   _____ to be treated with care.

2. When police receive a _____ from a person, they assume that
   person is guilty.

3. It is _____ to commit murder. It is a crime that is punishable by

   _____ injection.

4. Most people agree that there are many _____ to using
   the death penalty to punish criminals. Even people who support the death
   penalty believe it has imperfections.

5. It is believed that a person doesn't lose _____ while he
   or she is being put to death.

6. When authorities _____ the electrocution, it is common

   for the prisoner to experience _____ that cause the body
   to shake violently.

7. _____ in Florida, the death penalty is carried out

with a lethal injection. The drug is given to the prisoner _____
with a needle.

Be sure to visit <www.press.umich.edu/esl> for ideas on
related Web sites, videos, and other activities.

Put the Story Together: The Great Beyond

INTRODUCTION

Are you curious about your future? Do you believe that it is possible for someone to see what your future holds for you? Have you ever been to a fortune-teller? Have you ever had your palm read? In this unit, you will practice your speaking skills as you try to put together the parts of this story.

Exercise 11.1

Work in groups of 12.* Each student will have a piece of a story. Try to put the story together.

---

*If there are extra students, these students should be judges. The judges should listen to the story lines and decide if the 12 students have put themselves in the correct order or not. Conversely, if there are not 12 students, the teacher should participate, and perhaps one or two of the lines could be copied on a sheet of paper that could be placed on the floor in the correct position within the story. (See step 4.)

Step 1. Each student should look at one of these communication activities: 1, 11, 22, 25, 30, 35, 41, 51, 62, 74, 82, and 90.

Step 2. Write your activity number in the box and write your sentence on the line.

☐ _____

Step 3. You have one minute to read and memorize your piece of the story. You do not have to use the exact same words, but you do need to express the same idea.

Step 4. The twelve students should stand up and try to put themselves (their pieces of the story) in order by taking turns saying (not reading) their lines aloud.

Exercise 11.2

Work in small groups. Write another strip story like the one in exercise 11.1. Try to have a funny or surprising ending.

 Language Review

Match the definition in the right column with the correct word in the left column.

Vocabulary

___ 1. psychic

___ 2. departed

___ 3. flutter

___ 4. moaning

___ 5. emanates

___ 6. puzzled

___ 7. pauses

Definition

a. waits for a short time

b. a person who can see the future or communicate with people who have died

c. confused

d. gone

e. shake lightly

f. comes from; comes out of

g. making a low, deep sound

 Be sure to visit <www.press.umich.edu/esl> for ideas on related Web sites, videos, and other activities.

UNIT 12

The Punishment and the Crime

INTRODUCTION

This unit involves a very interesting question. If someone falsely accuses you of a crime, what punishment is appropriate for the accuser? Some would argue that it is not a very important crime. Of course people who have been falsely accused strenuously disagree.

Exercise 12.1

Read this court case involving an accusation of a very serious crime.

COURT CASE: A RAPE IN KENTUCKY

In 1988, Elizabeth Richardson accused Gary Nitsch of raping her. Richardson said that the rape occurred when Nitsch, a painter, was at her house for a painting job.

When Richardson reported the crime to police, she was able to describe Nitsch to a T. The police quickly arrested Nitsch based on Richardson's accurate description. In court, Richardson testified that Nitsch had raped her.

However, this story took a very bizarre turn when Richardson admitted to some of her friends that she had made up the story in order to get her husband's attention. In other words, her whole story was a hoax. According to Richardson's lawyer, making up this rape accusation against Nitsch was a spur-of-the-moment decision. Her marriage was in trouble, and her husband was often away on business. Her husband admitted that he was having affairs, and Richardson was desperate to get back at him.

This false accusation has affected both Richardson and Nitsch. Nitsch lost his job. His daughter dropped out of high school because she could not take the things that her fellow students were saying about her father being a rapist. His wife stopped going into town. When Nitsch goes into town, he tries to get someone else to drive him so he can sit way down in the seat so no one will recognize him. For Nitsch, this accusation has meant a huge financial and personal loss.

Richardson has had some serious problems as well as a direct result of this false accusation. She and her husband have divorced. She lost custody of her kids. She is working as a meat packer but does not make much money.

In court, Richardson admitted that she had lied about the rape by Nitsch. Richardson was convicted of perjury (lying under oath).

Exercise 12.2

If you were the judge, what punishment would you give to Richardson for committing perjury in this case? Be sure to consider the consequences that have happened to both people in this case as well as to their families.

_____

_____

_____

_____

_____

_____

_____

_____

_____

Exercise 12.3

Work in small groups of three to five members. Discuss your decision and your reasons. In the top row of the chart, write down your decision and your reasons for reaching this decision. In the next rows, write down your group members' decisions and one or two reasons that they give for their decisions.

Decision	Reasons for Decision
Yours	
_____ (name of group member)	
_____ (name of group member)	
_____ (name of group member)	
_____ (name of group member)	

Exercise 12.4

Read the judge's decision in communication activity 42. What is your reaction to the judge's sentence? Was it just? Was it too harsh? Was it too lenient?

_____

_____

Write two or three reasons to support your reaction.

_____

_____

_____

_____

_____

_____

Exercise 12.5

Work in small groups of three to five members to discuss your comments from exercise 12.4. What does your group think overall? Is there any consensus? Does the punishment fit the crime? Each group should try to agree on a unified group reaction to the judge's decision.

How many members in your group agree with the judge's decision? ___ of ___ (total number)

What are some reasons given by those who agree with the judge?

_____

_____

_____

_____

_____

What are some reasons given by those who disagree with the judge?

_____

_____

_____

_____

_____

Exercise 12.6

Some people believe that the punishment was just. They believe that a false accusation of a crime such as rape is extremely serious. Other people are concerned that the judge's decision will have a negative effect on other women who have been raped. Will people think that these women are just crying wolf? Will this decision make women who have actually been raped become more afraid to report the crime?

On the lines below, write any reactions or comments that you have for the above statements.

_____

_____

_____

_____

_____

_____

Exercise 12.7

In small groups of three to five, discuss your responses to exercise 12.6.

 Language Review

Read the key word or phrase (in bold) in the left column. Circle the letter of the choice that is related to the key word or phrase.

1. **accusation**   a. She said, "You did it."   b. She said, "You did well."

2. **rape**   a. quick division   b. sexual crime

3. **to a T**   a. quickly; with haste   b. exactly; with details

4. **bizarre**   a. strange   b. amazing

5. **lenient**   a. not strange   b. not strict

6. **make up a story**   a. invent a story   b. listen carefully to a story

7. **a hoax**   a. a false story   b. a brief story

8. **accurate**   a. exact   b. compassionate

9. **cry wolf**   a. not tell the truth   b. not admit your guilt

10. **consensus**   a. group agreement   b. individual right

11. **custody**   a. of a custom   b. of a child

12. **(be) convicted of**   a. something illegal   b. something difficult

13. **perjury**   a. telling a lie   b. telling some truths and some lies

14. **just decision**   a. time-consuming decision   b. fair decision

15. **oath**   a. "I swear this is true."   b. "I believe this is true."

16. **harsh**   a. strict; severe   b. compassionate; friendly

17. **the consequences**   a. rewards   b. results

18. **a desperate person**   a. The person wants something badly.   b. The person does not have friends.

19. **have an affair**   a. have secret meetings for sexual relations   b. make arrangements to sell company secrets

20. **take a turn**   a. change   b. decide

Be sure to visit <www.press.umich.edu/esl> for ideas on related Web sites, videos, and other activities.

UNIT 13

Corporal Punishment

INTRODUCTION

How did your parents discipline you? Did they spank you? Do you think that hitting a child is an appropriate form of discipline? This unit deals with issues related to disciplining children and adults.

Exercise 13.1

Write answers to these questions about corporal punishment.

1. What is corporal punishment?

_____

_____

_____

_____

_____

2. Is corporal punishment generally accepted today?

_____

_____

_____

_____

_____

3. How did your parents discipline you (i.e., teach you what's right and wrong)?

_____

_____

_____

_____

_____

_____

_____

Did you agree with this punishment then?

_____

Do you agree with this punishment now?

_____

4. What is your opinion of corporal punishment? Write reasons for your answer.

_____

_____

_____

_____

_____

_____

5. If you don't think corporal punishment is acceptable, what punishment do
    you suggest for

    a child who behaves badly at home?

    _____

    _____

    _____

    _____

    a child who behaves badly at school?

    _____

    _____

    _____

    _____

    a child who breaks the law?

    _____

    _____

    _____

    _____

an adult who breaks the law?

_____

_____

_____

_____

6. If you think corporal punishment is acceptable, is it permissible for these people to hit a child as punishment? Write yes or no and comment on your answer.

a. the child's parents

_____

_____

_____

_____

b. the child's teacher

_____

_____

_____

_____

c. the child's grandparents

_____

_____

_____

_____

Exercise 13.2

Work in groups. Discuss the topic of corporal punishment using the questions from exercise 13.1.

Exercise 13.3

In 1994, a crime happened that caused people to think about the use of corporal punishment. Read this excerpt, which explains the situation.

> In Singapore in 1994, an American teenager, Michael Fay, was accused of spray painting parked cars and having in his possession street signs that somebody stole. These acts are called vandalism, and they are considered crimes in Singapore. Michael Fay soon said that he committed the crimes, and he waited to hear the punishment.

Exercise 13.4

Do you agree that spray painting parked cars and having street signs that somebody stole are crimes? Write reasons for your answer.

_____

_____

_____

_____

_____

In Singapore, the common punishment for the crime of vandalism is to be hit with a cane, a four-foot-long, half-inch-wide piece of wood, one time or many times. If you were the Singapore government, what sentence (punishment) would you give to Michael Fay?

_____

_____

_____

Write two or three reasons for your opinion.

_____

_____

_____

_____

_____

Exercise 13.5

Work in small groups. Discuss your decision and your reasons. When you finish, read what punishment a prison martial arts expert gave Michael Fay in communication activity 26.

Exercise 13.6

In the United States, a common expression is "The punishment should fit the crime." What do you think this expression means? Write your guess here.

_____

_____

In your opinion, what punishment fits the following forms of crimes and misbehavior?

showing disrespect to your parents

_____

telling a lie

_____

saying hurtful things

_____

stealing

_____

hitting a person

_____

vandalizing public property

_____

using drugs

_____

murdering someone

_____

Exercise 13.7

Read the following story involving a child who misbehaved at school.

A nine-year-old boy often misbehaved in school and repeatedly caused trouble. "After all," he shouted, "what can they do about it?" He learned the answer to this question when a stern teacher spanked him. The boy ran home and told his parents. The parents eventually took the teacher to court.

"Some children can't learn without an occasional spanking," the teacher said. "If you won't discipline your child, the teacher has to. The spanking I gave him didn't even break the skin."

"That kind of discipline went out of style years ago," lawyers for the boy answered. "Children are people, and anyone who hits them is guilty the way that they would be if he or she hit an adult."

Exercise 13.8

If you were the judge, would you make the teacher pay money to the parents? _____

Write two or three reasons for your answer.

_____

_____

_____

_____

_____

_____

_____

_____

Exercise 13.9

Work in small groups. Discuss your decision and your reasons. When you finish, read the court's decision in communication activity 61.

Exercise 13.10

People who agree with corporal punishment say that it helps children and young adults to learn not to behave badly or to commit crimes. Do you think corporal punishment is a deterrent to bad behavior or crime? That is, do you think children or young adults behave correctly because they are afraid of being hit? Write reasons for your answer.

_____

_____

_____

_____

_____

_____

_____

_____

Exercise 13.11

In small groups, discuss your opinion and your reasons from exercise 13.10.

  Language Review

Use the vocabulary items in the box to complete the sentences.

discipline	fit	breaks the law
corporal punishment	vandalism	deterrent
behavior	court	commits
sentence	judge	acceptable

1. Most people agree that a person who _____ a crime
   should be punished.

2. After she listened to the arguments, the _____
   decided that the criminal's _____ should be five
   years in jail.

3. _____, the act of damaging or defacing public or private property, is a crime in many countries.

4. Many people believe that _____ is a _____ to crime; a person who is physically punished probably will not commit another crime.

5. Not all parents who believe it is _____ to _____ their children agree with hitting them. Some parents think that the best way to teach children is to take away a favorite toy or game.

6. If a person _____, that person must go to _____ to defend him- or herself.

Be sure to visit <<u>www.press.umich.edu/esl</u>> for ideas on related Web sites, videos, and other activities.

UNIT 14

Who Should Control Your Safety?

INTRODUCTION

When you ride or drive in a vehicle, do you wear a seat belt? Do you wear a seat belt every time you enter a vehicle? Is it appropriate for the government to force citizens to "buckle up"?

Exercise 14.1

Read the following statements and give your opinion. Circle 1 if you *agree strongly,* 2 if you *agree somewhat,* 3 if you are *not sure,* 4 if you *disagree somewhat,* and 5 if you *disagree strongly.* Then write your opinion about these statements. Be sure to include one or two reasons to explain your answer.

a. 1 2 3 4 5   My government must protect its people. (*Example:* The government maintains an army.)

_____

_____

_____

b. 1 2 3 4 5   My government must protect me from crime. (*Example:* The government maintains the police.)

_____

_____

_____

c. 1 2 3 4 5   It is OK for my government to make laws that stop me from hurting other people. (*Example:* I cannot hurt or kill someone.)

_____

_____

_____

d. 1 2 3 4 5   It is OK for my government to make laws that help me not to hurt myself. (*Example:* I have to wear a seat belt or a motorcycle helmet.)

_____

_____

_____

e. 1 2 3 4 5   If I want to do something that can hurt or kill me, it is OK for my government to stop me. (*Example:* I want to commit suicide.)

_____

_____

_____

f. 1 2 3 4 5   It is OK for my government to tell me what I can and cannot do with my body. (*Example:* I want to have an abortion.)

_____

_____

_____

Exercise 14.2

Work in groups to discuss your answers to exercise 14.1.

For which two questions do your group members have the widest variation in answers? ___ and ___ . On which statement do you disagree the most? ___ Why do you disagree on this statement?

_____

_____

_____

_____

_____

Exercise 14.3

Read the following story about a law that was passed in the state of Alabama.

On December 10, 1999, Alabama joined a long list of states that have passed laws that require drivers to wear safety belts. The Alabama law requires a driver to pay a fine of $25 if a police officer sees that he or she is not wearing a safety belt while driving. Some people who agree with this law say that it will not only help to save drivers' lives but that it will also encourage drivers to use child safety seats, which will in turn save children's lives as well. Some people who disagree with the law say that it is their choice to wear a safety belt or to drive without one and that no one—not even the government—has the right to tell them what to do with their bodies.

Exercise 14.4

If you were a government official in Alabama, would you require drivers to wear safety belts?

_____ Write two or three reasons for your decision.

_____

_____

_____

_____

_____

_____

_____

_____

Exercise 14.5

Work in small groups. Discuss your decision and your reasons.

Exercise 14.6

Answer questions 1–4. Then look at the statistics about wearing seat belts and write answers to questions 5 and 6.

1. Do you usually wear a seat belt when you are a passenger in a car? _____

   What about when you drive a car? _____

   Do you have any comments to explain your answers? _____

   _____

   _____

   _____

2. What percentage of people in vehicles in the United States do you think wear a seat belt?

_____ percent (You will find out the correct answer very soon.)

3. Why do some people insist on wearing a seat belt?

_____

_____

_____

_____

_____

4. Why do some people insist on NOT wearing a seat belt?

_____

_____

_____

_____

_____

_____

Seat Belt Effectiveness

Number of Motor Vehicle Deaths in 1998	41,471
National percentage of motor vehicle occupants wearing seat belts	69%
Number of lives saved by seat belt use	11,000
Projected number of lives saved if national percentage of seat belt use were 85%	16,200
Projected number of lives saved if national percentage of seat belt use were 100%	25,500

Source: Data from *Traffic Safety Facts 1998: Occupant Protection.* Washington, DC: National Highway Traffic Safety Administration, National Center for Statistics and Analysis, March 2000. <www.prevent.org>

How many people in the United States are killed in vehicle accidents in a typical year? In **1998, 41,471** occupants of motor vehicles were killed in motor vehicle crashes. About **55** percent of these occupants were **not** wearing seat belts.

In **1998,** the national seat belt use rate was **69** percent. This is just over two-thirds of all vehicle passengers. The NHTSA (National Highway Traffic Safety Administration) estimates that the wearing of seat belts by so many people saved more than **11,000** lives in that year.

While 69 percent of occupants with seat belts is a good percentage, the NHTSA estimates that if **85** percent of occupants wore seat belts, an additional **5,200** lives would be saved.

The NHTSA further concludes that if **all** passengers over age four wore seat belts, **9,300 additional** lives would be saved.

5. Do you know of governments that require you to wear safety belts? If so, what is the penalty if you do not wear a safety belt?

_____

_____

_____

_____

_____

6. Do you think that it is OK for a government to pass laws that require people to wear seat belts? To have air bags?

_____

_____

_____

_____

Exercise 14.7

Work in small groups. Discuss your answers to the questions above. Be sure to give reasons for your answers.

Exercise 14.8

Answer questions 1–4. Then look at the statistics about air bags and write answers to questions 5 and 6.

1. Have you ever driven or ridden in a car that had air bags? _____
   (Most new cars built after 2000 have driver air bags as standard; front seat passenger air bags are available in most new cars as well.)

2. Do you think it is really better to have air bags in a car? Why or why not?

   _____

   _____

   _____

3. Do you agree or disagree with the following statement? Air bags save lives, but air bags have actually killed some people. _____

   Why or why not? _____

   _____

   _____

   _____

4. Now study these statistics on air bags.

Air Bag Effectiveness as of 1999

Number of drivers saved by air bags	4,011
Number of passengers saved by air bags	747
Total confirmed air bag deaths as of October 1999	146

Source: National Highway Traffic Safety Administration <www.nhtsa.dot.gov/airbags/factsheets/numbers.html>

5. What is your reaction to these numbers?

   _____

   _____

_____
_____
_____
_____

6. Do you think that it is OK for a government to pass laws that require car manufacturers to install air bags in all new cars? Do you support this movement? Why or why not?

_____
_____
_____
_____
_____

Exercise 14.9

Work in small groups. Discuss your answers to the questions in exercise 14.8. Be sure to give reasons for your answers.

Exercise 14.10

Read the information about motorcycle helmet laws.

In the United States, only 4 of the 50 states allow motorcycle riders to ride without helmets. Of the remaining 46 states, 21 require all motorcyclists to wear helmets all of the time, and 20 others have helmet laws specifically for people under the age of 18. Many motorcycle riders feel they are being discriminated against (being treated unfairly) because they are "bikers," a word that is often used negatively. They argue that automobile drivers are not required to wear helmets, so it is not fair for them to be required to wear helmets. Riders around the world disagree with these laws and are trying to get more equal treatment. On the lines provided, write your opinion about helmets, helmet laws, and the rights of motorcyclists to make decisions about their own protection.

_____

_____

_____

_____

_____

_____

_____

_____

Exercise 14.11

Role Play

Scene: You are at a meeting of state lawmakers who are debating the issue of mandatory helmet laws. Each person will express an opinion in support of or against a law that would require all motorcycle drivers to wear helmets. In a nutshell, those who favor the law say that it will save lives while those who are against the law say that it is not right for the government to get so involved in people's daily lives.

Work in small groups (four or six people).
Each person should do ONE of the communication activities.
If there are four people, do 6, 19, 37, and 55.
If there are six people, do 6, 19, 37, 55, 66, and 81.

Step 1. What is your communication activity number? _____

Step 2. Write who you are on this line: _____

Step 3. What is your position about this proposed new law? Do you support it? Do you disagree with it? Why do you feel this way? Write your responses on the lines below.

_____

_____

_____

_____

_____

_____

_____

Step 4. Now work in groups. You are the person in step 2. Introduce yourself. Tell your opinion about the proposed new law. Be sure to give reasons to support your opinions. Feel free to ask the other members questions or to comment on their statements during the discussion.

 ## Language Review

Use the vocabulary items in the box to complete the sentences.

argue	fine	law	protect
citizen	helmets	mandatory	safety belts
discriminated	injured	penalty	statistics

1. In many states, it is _____ for motorcyclists to wear

   _____ when they ride.

2. Some motorcyclists feel they are _____ against, or

   treated unfairly, because they ride motorcycles.

3. People who agree with the helmet _____ believe

   that helmets will _____ riders from serious harm.

4. _____ show that the average _____

   agrees that motorcycle riders should wear helmets because helmets can

   save lives.

5. Riders who disobey the law have to pay a _____.

6. When automobile drivers don't wear _____ , there is

a good chance they will be _____ .

Bonus question: What does "in a nutshell" mean? _____

Be sure to visit <<u>www.press.umich.edu/esl</u>> for ideas on
related Web sites, videos, and other activities.

More Practice with Proverbs

INTRODUCTION

Proverb: "Give him an inch, he'll take a mile." What do you think this proverb means? A proverb is a brief saying that teaches a lesson. The proverb above means that some people try to take advantage of your niceness or hospitality. For example, you have a good collection of tools, and your neighbor needs to borrow a hammer. Since you are a nice person, you offer to lend your neighbor a hammer. Instead of saying "Thank you," your neighbor says, "OK, that's good . . . and can you lend me a saw and some nails, too?" You offered your neighbor something (= an inch), but then your neighbor got greedy and tried to get more from you (= a mile). Proverbs are interesting because they reveal so much about a culture's values or lack thereof.

Exercise 15.1

Read these eight proverbs. Try to guess the meaning of each proverb. Write your guesses on the lines.

a. You may lead a horse to water, but you can't make it drink.

_____

_____

b. Don't judge a book by its cover.

_____

_____

c. If you fall off a horse, get right back on.

_____

_____

d. All that glitters is not gold.

_____

_____

e. People who live in glass houses shouldn't throw stones.

_____

_____

f. Don't play with fire or you might get burned.

_____

_____

g. Let bygones be bygones.

_____

_____

h. It takes two to tango.

_____

_____

Exercise 15.2

Now work in groups of four students. Take turns discussing your guesses about the meanings of the proverbs in exercise 15.1. Student 1 should do a and b, student 2 should do c and d, student 3 should do e and f, and student 4 should do g and h. Give reasons for what you have written as your guesses.

Exercise 15.3

After you finish exercises 15.1 and 15.2, in groups of four students, check your answers in the following communication activities. Each student in the group will be responsible for reading the answer with the correct meaning of two proverbs.

Student 1 should read communication activity 16, student 2 can read communication activity 34, student 3 can read communication activity 58, and student 4 can read communication activity 79.

Take turns explaining in your own words what the correct meanings of these proverbs are. Do not just read the words from the back of the book. Try to use your own words as much as possible.

Exercise 15.4

Write a situation that explains one of the proverbs in exercise 15.1. Write the proverb on the line after the situation.

Situation:

_____

_____

_____

_____

_____

Proverb:

_____

Exercise 15.5

Work in small groups (a group of three students is best). Take turns reading your situation aloud (or telling your situation if you can remember all the details). After a group member describes a situation, the others should try to guess what the proverb is.

Exercise 15.6

Write down a proverb in your native language or another language you know. Translate the words (literal translation) and see if anyone from a different language background can guess the meaning of the proverb. Then work with a native speaker to see if you can find an English proverb that has a similar meaning. (Sometimes the translations will be very similar, but sometimes they will be very different.)

In another language:

_____

_____

Literal translation:

_____

_____

Equivalent English proverb:

_____

_____

Language Review

Read the key word (in bold) in the left column. Circle the letter of the choice that is related to the key word.

1. **refuse**   a. say yes   b. say no

2. **succeed**   a. do well   b. do poorly

3. **discouraged** a. without hope   b. without much money

4. **glitters**   a. shines; sparkles b. increases; exceeds

5. **bygones**   a. from the past   b. from right now

6. **equivalent**   a. similar   b. beautiful

Be sure to visit <www.press.umich.edu/esl> for ideas on related Web sites, videos, and other activities.

Faith Healing: Trust the Doctor or Trust God?

INTRODUCTION

This unit presents a case involving the validity of two parents' decision regarding their children's health. Their decision was based on their religious beliefs, but was this a logical decision?

Exercise 16.1

Who is responsible for a person's well-being? Read the following situations and choose if the responsibility to act is with the individual (I), the parents (P), the government (GOV), or god (G). Circle the letter(s) that best show(s) your opinion. In other words, who has the right to make this decision? Remember that more than one answer is possible. Be sure to include one or two reasons to explain your answer.

a. I   P   G   GOV

I am 15 years old and unhappy, and I want to end my life.

_____

_____

_____

b. I   P   G   GOV

I am 25 years old, and I want to have an operation to change the shape of my nose.

_____

_____

_____

c. I   P   G   GOV

My 5-year-old daughter has cancer. The doctors say she will die a painful death.

_____

_____

_____

d. I   P   G   GOV

I am a 62-year-old woman who has Alzheimer's disease. I don't know my family when I see them, and I want to die because I am very sad.

_____

_____

_____

e. I   P   G   GOV

I am a 30-year-old man. I have had a lot of pain in my chest for six months, but I don't want to go to the doctor because I am afraid.

_____

_____

_____

f. I   P   G   GOV

I am a 40-year-old man. I have AIDS. I am not responding to my medication, and my doctors agree that I have less than two months to live. They also believe that I will probably go blind and maybe deaf before I die. In addition, I will probably not be aware of who I am and will become paralyzed (will lose control of all bodily functions, including breathing) and may require a breathing machine. I would like to die while I am able to control my own destiny by taking some pills to end my life peacefully.

_____

_____

_____

Exercise 16.2

Work in groups to discuss your answers to exercise 16.1.

For which two questions do your group members have the widest variation in answers? ___ and ___

On which statement do you disagree the most? ___ Why do you disagree on this statement?

_____

_____

_____

_____

_____

_____

_____

Exercise 16.3

Read this situation involving a very ill child and her religious parents.

In Hollidaysburg, Pennsylvania, Dennis and Lorie Nixon were very worried about their 16-year-old daughter, Shannon, who had diabetes, a life-threatening disorder in which a person's body cannot produce enough insulin or cannot use insulin effectively. They decided not to take the girl to a doctor for treatment but chose to have Dennis's father, Charles Nixon, a pastor of the Faith Tabernacle Congregation, pray for the girl and anoint her with oil (put a small amount of oil on her as a blessing) in an effort to keep her alive. In the end, Shannon died of complications from diabetes. Shannon was the second child of the Nixon's 10 children to die because she received religious attention instead of medical attention.

The Nixons were arrested and had to go to court to defend their decision to act as they did. They faced a charge of involuntary manslaughter, the unlawful killing of a person without choosing to do it.

Exercise 16.4

If you were on the jury, how would you rule (guilty or not guilty)?

_____

If you think the Nixons are guilty, what punishment do you think the Nixons should receive?

_____

_____

_____

_____

_____

Write two or three reasons for your decision.

_____

_____

_____

_____

_____

_____

_____

Exercise 16.5

Work in small groups. Discuss your decision and your reasons. When you finish, read communication activity 87 to find out the jury's decision.

Exercise 16.6

Role Play

Scene: This is a discussion of the people involved in this case.

Work in groups of four, six, or eight members.

Each person should do ONE of the communication activities.

If there are four people, do 4, 68, 28, and 80.

If there are six people, do 4, 68, 28, 80, 44, and 57.

If there are eight people, do 4, 68, 28, 80, 44, 57, 15, and 36.

Step 1.   What is your communication activity number? _____

Step 2. Write who you are on this line: _____

Step 3. What are your feelings about what happened? Why do you feel this way? Write your responses on these lines.

_____

_____

_____

_____

_____

_____

_____

_____

_____

_____

_____

_____

Step 4. Now work in groups. You are the person in step 2. Introduce yourself. Tell your opinion of the problem. Tell the group what you think should happen and why. Feel free to ask the other members questions or to comment on their statements during the discussion.

Language Review

Match the definition in the right column with the correct word or phrase in the left column.

___ 1. Alzheimer's disease   a. illegal

___ 2. arrest   b. reasonable; something that makes sense

___ 3. be aware of   c. disease that affects the ability to remember

___ 4. diabetes   d. something naturally or legally given to someone

___ 5. faith

___ 6. heal   e. be charged with a crime by the police

___ 7. regarding   f. relating to God

___ 8. paralyzed   g. know about something

___ 9. religious   h. very dangerous disorder of the body

___ 10. right   i. trust in something or someone, usually in God

___ 11. logical   j. unable to move part of one's body

___ 12. unlawful   k. get better; change from sick to well

   l. about; dealing with (a topic)

Be sure to visit <www.press.umich.edu/esl> for ideas on related Web sites, videos, and other activities.

The Abortion Debate

INTRODUCTION

Abortion is legal in many countries around the world. In some countries, abortion is still illegal. Abortion has been legal in the United States for about 30 years. However, for many people here, abortion is still a very controversial issue. Is it murder of an unborn child? Or is it simply a woman controlling her own body?

Exercise 17.1

Read the following situations and indicate your reaction by circling 1 if you *agree strongly,* 2 if you *agree somewhat,* 3 if you are *not sure,* 4 if you *disagree somewhat,* and 5 if you *disagree strongly.* Then write your opinion about these statements. On the lines after each statement, write one or two reasons to explain your opinion.

a. 1 2 3 4 5 Abortion is acceptable when the woman's physical health is in danger.

_____

_____

_____

_____

_____

b. 1 2 3 4 5 Abortion is acceptable when the woman's mental health is in danger.

_____

_____

_____

_____

_____

c. 1 2 3 4 5 Abortion is acceptable when there is evidence that the baby may be physically handicapped.

_____

_____

_____

_____

_____

d. 1 2 3 4 5 Abortion is acceptable when there is evidence that the baby may be mentally impaired.

_____

_____

_____

_____

_____

e. 1 2 3 4 5   Abortion is acceptable when the pregnancy was caused by rape or incest.

_____

_____

_____

_____

_____

f. 1 2 3 4 5   Abortion is an act of murder and is never acceptable.

_____

_____

_____

_____

_____

g. 1 2 3 4 5   The father of an unborn child has the right to tell the mother not to get an abortion.

_____

_____

_____

_____

_____

h. 1 2 3 4 5   Abortion is acceptable when it is done in a way that does not harm the mother.

_____

_____

_____

_____

_____

i. 1 2 3 4 5   An abortion in the early stages of pregnancy is more acceptable than one in the later stages of pregnancy.

_____

_____

_____

_____

_____

Exercise 17.2

Work in small groups. Discuss your responses to the statements in exercise 17.1.

Exercise 17.3

A very famous case involving the abortion controversy was argued in 1973. Read this summary, which highlights the most important points of the case.

> In 1973, Jane Roe, an unmarried resident of the state of Texas, learned that she was pregnant and wanted to terminate her pregnancy by abortion. However, at that time, Texas law prohibited abortions except when they would save the pregnant woman's life.

When arguing the famous case before the Supreme Court, a case now referred to as *Roe v. Wade*, Jane Roe's attorney cited several reasons why the Texas law was unacceptable according to her client. Some of the reasons follow.

- The law is unconstitutional because it violates a woman's right to determine to continue or terminate a pregnancy.
- A doctor does not know whether he or she can perform an abortion only when death is imminent or whether abortion is also allowable when the woman's life would be shortened. The doctor doesn't know if the death must be certain or if an increase in probability of the woman's death is also an acceptable reason for abortion.
- In the absence of legal abortions, women often resort to illegal abortions, which certainly carry risks of death.
- If the pregnancy would result in the birth of a deformed or otherwise handicapped child, the woman has no relief.
- If the pregnancy is a result of rape or incest, the woman has no relief.
- There are many schools that require a young woman to quit if she becomes pregnant.
- A woman is often forced to quit her job as a result of her pregnancy and is not eligible for unemployment benefits because she is not qualified to work.

The United States Supreme Court was asked to decide this case.

Exercise 17.4

Write your response to this case. If you were a Supreme Court justice, how would you rule? Give reasons to support your answer.

_____

_____

_____

_____

Exercise 17.5

Work in small groups. Discuss your opinion of this important case. When you finish, turn to communication activity 7 to read the Supreme Court's decision.

Exercise 17.6

Read this brief passage about an abortion option available in France and other parts of Europe that has generated interest and attempts at legalization in the United States.

The prescription drug RU-486 provides medically induced abortions to women who are in the earliest stages of pregnancy. The drug, which has been available in France since 1988 and is becoming more widely available in other European countries, offers women the opportunity to have an abortion without using the traditional surgical methods.

A woman wishing to have an abortion before the seventh week of her pregnancy visits her doctor, who gives her a small pill to take. In as little as 4 hours or as many as 72 hours, the woman finds a comfortable place to lie down and then vaginally inserts four tablets of another medication that causes her uterus to contract and expel its lining and the sac that contains the embryo. There is a chance of cramping and bleeding, possibly severe.

People who oppose the use of the pill argue that it makes abortions too simple and easy and that women might turn to the pill before considering other options. People who support the use of the pill do so because it will make abortion more accessible and private while making it harder for antiabortion activists to identify—and potentially harm—women who receive abortions and doctors who perform them.

The United States Food and Drug Administration (FDA) has the responsibility to approve or deny the marketing of RU-486 based on its safety and effectiveness.

Exercise 17.7

If you were the FDA, how would you rule? Should women have access to this controversial drug? Give reasons for your opinion.

_____

_____

_____

_____

_____

_____

_____

_____

Exercise 17.8

Work in small groups. Discuss your opinion and reasons. When you finish, read the FDA's decision in communication activity 48.

Exercise 17.9

The abortion controversy has brought passionate responses—and even violence—from people in recent years. Many people who oppose abortion feel justified in threatening and harming abortion clinics and the doctors who perform abortions. Some people even believe that killing a doctor in the interest of saving an unborn child is acceptable. Read the statements below and write your responses on the lines.

For every 1,000 women of childbearing age, 35 are estimated to have an

induced abortion each year. _____

_____

_____

_____

"Sometimes you have to use force to stop people from killing innocent children." _____

_____

_____

_____

"We shouldn't stand by with our hands in our pockets and watch . . . our wives kill our unborn children." _____

_____

_____

_____

Exercise 17.10

Work in small groups. Discuss your responses to the statements in exercise 17.9.

Exercise 17.11

Role Play

Scene: Several people at a community meeting are discussing whether or not abortion should be legalized.

Work in small groups (four, five, or six people).

Each person should do ONE of the communication activities.

If there are four people, do 5, 23, 54, and 71.

If there are five people, do 5, 23, 54, 71, and 85.

If there are six people, do 5, 23, 54, 71, 85, and 13.

Step 1. What is your communication activity number? _____

Step 2. Write who you are on this line: _____

_____

Step 3. What are your feelings about what happened? Why do you feel this way? Write your responses on these lines.

_____

_____

_____

_____

_____

_____

_____

_____

_____

_____

_____

_____

Step 4. Now work in groups. You are the person in step 2. Introduce yourself. Tell your opinion of the problem. Tell the group what you think should happen and why. Feel free to ask the other members questions or to comment on their statements during the discussion.

Language Review

Match the definition in the right column with the correct word or phrase in the left column.

Vocabulary	Definition
_____ 1. abortion	a. right or valid
_____ 2. impaired	b. the unborn young before eight weeks of development
_____ 3. incest	
_____ 4. stage	c. turn to
_____ 5. controversy	d. against the basic rules of the United States
_____ 6. terminate	e. end
_____ 7. cite	f. a period of time
_____ 8. unconstitutional	g. lessened in strength or quality; harmed
_____ 9. imminent	h. the intentional ending of a pregnancy
_____ 10. resort to	i. sexual relations with a member of one's family
_____ 11. induced	j. marked by the expression of opposing views
_____ 12. embryo	k. give as proof or support of something
_____ 13. fetus	l. about to happen
_____ 14. justified	m. cause to occur
	n. the unborn young after eight weeks of development

Be sure to visit <www.press.umich.edu/esl> for ideas on related Web sites, videos, and other activities.

Put the Story Together: A Van Full of Penguins

INTRODUCTION

In this unit, you will practice putting together the pieces of a story. However, each person will have only one piece of the story. Can you figure out the correct sequencing of the pieces?

Exercise 18.1

Work in groups of eight.* Each student will have a piece of a story. Try to put the story together.

Step 1. Each student should look at one of these communication activities: 8, 18, 33, 46, 67, 77, 84, and 91.

Step 2. Write your activity number in the box and write your sentence on the line.

> [ ] _____

Step 3. You have one minute to read and memorize your piece of the story. You do not have to use the exact same words, but you do need to express the same idea.

Step 4. The eight students should stand up and try to put themselves (their pieces of the story) in order by taking turns saying (not reading) their lines aloud.

Exercise 18.2

Work in small groups. Write another strip story like the one in exercise 18.1. Try to have a funny or surprising ending.

---

*If there are extra students, these students should be judges. The judges should listen to the story lines and decide if the eight students have put themselves in the correct order or not. Conversely, if there are not eight students, the teacher should participate, and perhaps one or two of the lines could be copied on a sheet of paper that could be placed on the floor in the correct position within the story. (See step 4.)

Language Review

Match the definition in the right column with the correct word or phrase in the left column.

Vocabulary	*Definition*
___ 1. penguin	a. in the direction of
___ 2. deliver	b. relax; take it easy for a minute
___ 3. be supposed to	c. enter a bus or an airplane
___ 4. calm down	d. a bird that lives in cold climates
___ 5. route	e. After something is used, a portion of it remains.
___ 6. get on	
___ 7. plead (with someone)	f. beg; ask very strongly
___ 8. toward	g. take something to another place
___ 9. have (thing) left over	h. the way or path
___ 10. catch up with	i. reach the same level or position as someone else
	j. should happen or expected to happen

Be sure to visit <<u>www.press.umich.edu/esl</u>> for ideas on related Web sites, videos, and other activities.

The 10 Most Important Events in History

INTRODUCTION

What events changed our world forever? This unit discusses some of these historic events and how they were crucial in the development of humankind.

Exercise 19.1

Encyclopedia Britannica is one of the leading encyclopedias. In 1993, as part of its 225th anniversary celebration, the editors of *Encyclopedia Britannica* compiled a list of the 10 most significant events or discoveries in the history of the world. Try to come up with the 10 events or discoveries that made the editors' list. Write your answers below. Remember, you should not list anything that occurred after 1993.

1. _____

2. _____

3. _____

4. _____

5. _____

6. _____

7. _____

8. _____

9. _____

10. _____

Exercise 19.2

Now work with a partner or in small groups. Take turns reading the events on your lists. Discuss which ones your group believes are the most likely to be on the editors' list. Write your new list on the lines below.

1. _____

2. _____

3. _____

4. _____

5. _____

6. _____

7. _____

8. _____

9. _____

10. _____

Exercise 19.3

As a class activity, a leader or two leaders from each group should present their group's compilation to the whole class. It might be a good idea to make some sort of visual list (e.g., write on newsprint with markers or write on the blackboard). Discuss which of these events are probably on the editors' list.

Exercise 19.4

Work in groups of 5 or 10. Each student will find out one or two of the most important events on the editors' list and report this information to the group.

>   If there are 10 members, each student should choose ONE communication activity.
>   If there are 5 members, each student should choose TWO communication activities.

(It is important to make sure that two or more students do not select the same communication activity.)

Communication activities: 10, 21, 38, 43, 50, 59, 63, 69, 73, 76.

Find your communication activities and write the events on the lines below. If there are 10 members, you will use only the first space below. If there are 5 members, you will do two events and use both spaces below.

Communication activity number: _____

Event: _____

_____

Communication activity number: _____

Event: _____

_____

Homework: Go to the Internet or a reference book in the library and find out some basic information about the historic event that you have. When was it? Is there a person's name associated with it? Where did it happen? Write the information on the lines that follow. At the next class meeting, you will have to talk about the historic event for 30 to 60 seconds.

Event: _____

Information: _____

_____

_____

_____

_____

_____

_____

_____

_____

_____

_____

_____

_____

_____

_____

_____

(If there are five students in the group, you should list a second event and information about that event on the lines that follow.)

Event: _____

Information: _____

_____

_____

_____

_____

_____

_____

_____

_____

_____

_____

_____

_____

_____

_____

Exercise 19.5

In your group or as a class, make a list of the 10 events from the editors' list by taking turns telling the events in your communication activity from exercise 19.4. The order of these events does not matter for now. If you do not understand something that a speaker has said, ask for clarification. Ask for the correct spellings of any words and terms that are not familiar to you.

1. _____

2. _____

3. _____

4. _____

5. _____

6. _____

7. _____

8. _____

9. _____

10. _____

Exercise 19.6

Now take turns telling why your event is important in any discussion of the history of the world. You may use the information given in the communication activity and any information that you have gathered from an encyclopedia, another reference book, or the Internet. Again, if you do not understand something that the speaker has said, be sure to ask for clarification.

Exercise 19.7

This is the most difficult exercise in this unit. Rank the 10 activities from the master list in exercise 19.5. Put your list in the chart below with your most important event at the top of the list. (For the time being, do not write anything in the two columns on the far right.)

Your Ranking	Events	Your Group's Ranking	Editors' Ranking
1.			
2.			
3.			
4.			
5.			
6.			
7.			
8.			
9.			
10.			

Exercise 19.8

Now work in small groups. Discuss your rankings and come up with a group consensus for the order of the 10 historic events. When you have finished, everyone in your group should put the group's ranking in the column labeled "Your Group's Ranking."

Exercise 19.9

When you have finished compiling the consensus for exercise 19.8 and have concluded all discussions on your group ranking, turn to communication activity 83 to find out the editors' ranking. Use the information in the communication activity to fill out the far right column labeled "Editors' Ranking." Which group in your class or which individual student was the most accurate in matching the editors' ranking?

Exercise 19.10

a. Choose what you consider to be one of the very important events from the list that you created in exercise 19.1, or from another student's list for that exercise, that did not make the editors' list. Write a short explanation of why you believe that this event should have made the list. Be sure to give at least three reasons to back up your choice of event.

Event: _____

Reasons: _____

_____

_____

_____

_____

_____

_____

_____

b. Choose one of the events from the editors' list that you believe should not have been included in the top 10 events. Write a short explanation of why you believe that this event should not have made the list. Be sure to give at least three reasons to back up your answer.

Event: _____

Reasons: _____

_____

_____

_____

_____

_____

_____

Exercise 19.11

Work in small groups. Discuss your responses to parts a and b of exercise 19.10.

 ### Language Review

Read the key word or phrase (in bold) in the left column. Circle the letter of the choice that is related to the key word or phrase.

1. **development**	a. growth	b. destruction
2. **crucial**	a. very important	b. very interesting
3. **rank**	a. put in order	b. make a list
4. **come up with**	a. describe	b. produce
5. **gather**	a. distribute	b. collect
6. **accurate**	a. stop a sickness	b. exact
7. **compile**	a. put together	b. choose the best
8. **for the time being**	a. for the future	b. for the present
9. **make it on a list**	a. create a list	b. include in a list
10. **label**	a. the size	b. the name
11. **significant**	a. entertaining	b. important
12. **visual**	a. related to seeing	b. related to knowing

Be sure to visit <www.press.umich.edu/esl> for ideas on related Web sites, videos, and other activities.

UNIT 20

Playing God: Genetic Engineering

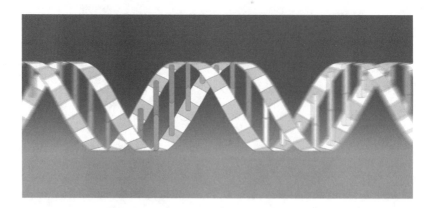

INTRODUCTION

Medical science has seen an amazing number of innovations. One of the most promising involves our chromosomes. The chromosomes that control our hair color, our height, and our likelihood of developing certain diseases have been identified. Scientists can alter some of these chromosomes already and will be able to do so for many others in the near future. This unit discusses whether or not this ability is a good thing.

Exercise 20.1

Read the following statements and indicate your reaction by circling 1 if you *agree* strongly, 2 if you *agree somewhat*, 3 if you are *not sure*, 4 if you *disagree somewhat*, and 5 if you *disagree strongly.* Then write your opinion about these statements. Be sure to include one or two reasons to explain your opinion.

a. 1   2   3   4   5   If I knew my baby were going to grow up to be a criminal, I would choose to change it genetically.

_____

_____

_____

b. 1   2   3   4   5   It is OK for doctors to use genetic engineering technology to change a baby's eye color according to the parents' wishes.

_____

_____

_____

c. 1   2   3   4   5   If I could, I would choose the sex of my baby.

_____

_____

_____

d. 1   2   3   4   5   If I knew my baby were going to be born with mental or physical retardation, I would choose to change it genetically.

_____

_____

_____

e. 1   2   3   4   5   If I knew my baby were going to be born a gay or a lesbian, I would choose to change it genetically.

_____

_____

_____

f. 1   2   3   4   5   People have the right to decide what a "perfect" baby is
                          and to create it if they are able.

_____

_____

_____

g. 1   2   3   4   5   If I could, I would want to know what diseases I might
                          suffer later in life (because I carry genes for those dis-
                          eases).

_____

_____

_____

h. 1   2   3   4   5   Changing human genes is against God's wishes.

_____

_____

_____

Exercise 20.2

Work in small groups to discuss your responses to the statements in exercise
20.1. For which two items do your group members have the widest variation in
answers?

___ and ___ Which statement is the most controversial? ___

Why is it controversial? _____

_____

_____

Exercise 20.3

Read this brief passage on genetic engineering.

> Genetic engineering is the practice of isolating human genes and making changes—improvements to them. Scientists have found many uses for genetic engineering, including curing diseases and doing away with inherited birth defects.
>
> People in favor of genetic engineering argue that it provides an excellent opportunity for doctors and scientists to help people live longer and to predict potential problems with unborn babies. Opponents of genetic engineering suggest that this technology allows doctors and scientists to "play God" with human life.

Exercise 20.4

Have you ever heard of genetic engineering? (If not, ask a native speaker or find some information in English about this topic.) Do you think that genetic engineering is a good idea? Why or why not?

_____

_____

_____

_____

_____

_____

Now take the opposing view. What do you think are two or three reasons to support that view?

_____

_____

_____

_____

_____

_____

Exercise 20.5

Read the situations and questions about potential problems with genetic engineering.

a. One opponent of genetic engineering asks, "What if we get rid of heart disease, Alzheimer's disease, and cancer? What on earth are we going to die of?"

What is your response to this question?

_____

_____

_____

_____

_____

_____

b. It is possible that genetic engineering could someday be used against us. Because a drop of blood contains all of a person's genetic information, a potential employer or an insurance company could use the information gathered from a DNA test to learn if someone is at risk of getting a life-threatening disease.

What is your response to this statement?

_____

_____

_____

_____

_____

_____

c. Research suggests that our genes can predict our tendency to commit violent crimes. One behavior geneticist says that "we already have a true genetic marker, detectable before birth, that predicts violence . . . [this] high-risk marker is: being male."

What is your response to this statement?

_____

_____

_____

_____

_____

_____

Exercise 20.6

Have you changed the opinion about genetic engineering that you expressed in the first part of exercise 20.4? Write reasons for your answer.

_____

_____

_____

_____

_____

_____

_____

_____

_____

_____

_____

Exercise 20.7

Read this true story of a woman with a serious medical problem.

Anna Fisher is surrounded by female family members who have been diagnosed with—or who have died of—cancer. Her grandmother and her mother both died of cancer, her aunt was diagnosed with ovarian tumors, and her five cousins all developed breast cancer.

In 1990, Anna's doctors told her that she had ovarian cancer, and she of course was not surprised. Anna had surgery and aggressive chemotherapy, a treatment that required cancer-fighting liquid chemicals to be injected into Anna's system.

Soon after the operation, doctors told Anna about the likely genetic connection between ovarian cancer and breast cancer. Although they had not found breast cancer in Anna's body, doctors suggested that Anna have both her breasts surgically removed in an effort to prevent her from getting the disease and to possibly save her life. This recommendation was made because Mary-Claire King, a geneticist at the University of California, Berkeley, had discovered that there was a single gene that connected the two types of cancer. King found a similar pattern of markers on the chromosomes from women in families with high incidences of cancer.

Anna joined King's study and found that she carried the same pattern of markers on her chromosomes. She faced an agonizing decision: Should she have an operation to remove both her breasts? King says that 5 percent to 10 percent of breast cancer cases are the inherited type. Carriers have an 85 percent chance of developing breast cancer by age 65. (This would mean that there might be 500,000 women in the United States who either already have or will develop breast cancer because of their genes.)

Exercise 20.8

If you were Anna, what decision would you make?

Exercise 20.9

Compare answers with a partner. Then read communication activity 24 to find out Anna's decision.

Language Review

Match the definition in the right column with the correct word or phrase in the left column.

____ 1. retardation
____ 2. isolating
____ 3. inherit
____ 4. potential
____ 5. tendency
____ 6. risk
____ 7. chemotherapy
____ 8. remove
____ 9. opponent
____ 10. defect
____ 11. diagnose
____ 12. likelihood
____ 13. incidence
____ 14. agonizing

a. take away; take out

b. danger

c. possible

d. separating; setting apart

e. lack of normal mental or physical ability ("slowness")

f. receive biologically from a parent or grandparent

g. chance that something will happen

h. medical treatment using chemicals to treat cancer

i. flaw; error

j. person who is against something

k. examine (to find out if something is wrong)

l. probability of behaving or thinking in a certain way

m. number of cases (e.g., of a disease)

n. causing great pain or mental anguish

Be sure to visit <www.press.umich.edu/esl> for ideas on related Web sites, videos, and other activities.

Communication Activities

Communication Activity 1

Write this line on page 71: Wide-eyed, Tatiana responds, "Grandmother? Is that you?"

Communication Activity 2

Write this line on page 45: "I have a broken finger."

Communication Activity 3

Sindy Allen: You are 18 years old. You are a student at the University of Nevada in Las Vegas. You work the night shift at a health food store. Your opinion is that the bottle cap is yours because you found it. You do not want to share the money. You believe that whoever finds something owns it.

Communication Activity 4

You are the judge in this case.

Communication Activity 5

You are an unmarried pregnant woman. You cannot have this baby because you do not have a job and are not capable or ready to take care of a child.

Communication Activity 6

You are an adult motorcycle rider who has seen a few motorcycle crashes over the years. In fact, one of your best friends was killed in a motorcycle crash. The police said that if your friend had been wearing a helmet, he probably would have survived the crash. You support new laws to make sure that all motorcycle drivers wear helmets.

Communication Activity 7

The Supreme Court held that a woman's right to an abortion fell within the right to privacy protected by the Fourteenth Amendment of the Constitution. The decision gave a woman complete control over her body during the first trimester (three months) of her pregnancy and provided different levels of personal/state responsibility for the second and third trimesters. In summary, the *Roe v. Wade* case resulted in the legalization of abortion in the United States.

Communication Activity 8

The bus driver said to the van driver, "Hey, where are you going? I gave you a hundred dollars to take the penguins to the zoo."

Communication Activity 9

Write this line on page 45: "And when I do the same to my cheek, it's also painful."

Communication Activity 10

the creation of the electrical telegraph and telephone

Communication Activity 11

Write this line on page 71: Tatiana pauses. "Grandmother, I have just one question."

Communication Activity 12

Topic: Education. You will write about education in the past, education in the present, and education in the future.
Here are some possible questions and suggestions to help you write your descriptions.

1. Did/Do/Will most people go to school?
2. What did/do/will schools look like?
3. Describe the teachers.
4. Describe the use of any extra machines.
5. How long did/do/will students go to school each day?
6. How many days a week did/do/will students go to school?

Communication Activity 13

You are a woman who had an abortion in the past. Unfortunately, there were complications from the operation that left you unable to have children.

Communication Activity 14

a. *Actions speak louder than words.* This proverb means that what you do is more important than what you say. For example, if person A promises again and again to help person B paint his house but doesn't do it, person B might say, "I'm not going to listen to your promises. Actions speak louder than words!"

b. *All's well that ends well.* This proverb means that a bad situation is not really so bad as long as it has a good ending or final result. If the end of the story is good, it doesn't really matter that there were some difficulties along the way.

Communication Activity 15

You are Shannon, the sick daughter who will die.

Communication Activity 16

a. *You may lead a horse to water, but you can't make it drink.* When you "make" someone do something, you force him or her to do it. This proverb means that you can create a perfect situation for someone to do something, but if the person doesn't want to do it, you can't force him or her to do it. My best friend wanted to get married, so she bought a dress and invited friends to her wedding, but her boyfriend refused to marry her. So, I said, "You have to remember that you may lead a horse to water, but you can't make it drink."

b. *Don't judge a book by its cover.* This proverb means that you can't form an opinion about a book (or a person) without knowing about what's inside of it (or him or her). For example, if I say that I think someone is stupid without speaking to him or her, my friend might say, "You don't know for sure. You can't judge a book by its cover."

Communication Activity 17

Judy Richardson: You are 45 years old. You work the morning shift at a health food store. You yourself admit—and everyone who works with you knows—that you are basically addicted to Pepsi and that you keep your bottles of Pepsi in a certain place at the store. When you heard that Allen had found the winning cap, you knew that it was a bottle of Pepsi that you had bought and put there earlier.

Communication Activity 18

The bus driver agreed to the plan. The van driver happily gave the bus driver the money, and then all the penguins got on the bus.

Communication Activity 19

You are an adult motorcycle rider who has ridden motorcycles for almost 20 years. You have never seen a motorcycle accident. None of your many friends who drive motorcycles have been involved in any accidents. You ride a motorcycle because you like the freedom that you feel. You like feeling the wind on your face. You don't like helmets, and you really don't like the government telling you that you have to wear a helmet.

Communication Activity 20

Write this line on page 45: "What did the specialist say?" the doctor asked.

Communication Activity 21

the French Revolution and Napoleonic Wars

Communication Activity 22

Write this line on page 71: "When did you learn to speak English?"

Communication Activity 23

You are a pregnant woman who has been advised that your pregnancy could kill you. Your doctor strongly recommends an abortion. You have mixed feelings, but you do not want to die. (Your husband is in this conversation, too.)

Communication Activity 24

Anna Fisher's common sense told her that her risk of developing breast cancer was too high to ignore. She had an operation to remove both her breasts. She said, "I did the best I could to prevent breast cancer. I hope it will be enough."

Communication Activity 25

Write this line on page 71: The psychic's eyelids flutter, her hands float above the table, and she begins moaning.

Communication Activity 26

A judge sentenced Michael Fay to have a prison martial arts expert give him four powerful strokes with a wet rattan cane. Michael Fay's father believed that Americans would be shocked by this sentence and that the U.S. government would try to change the decision, so he told all the American newspapers about it. To his surprise, Americans who are tired of crime agreed with the Singapore government. The case caused public officials in Sacramento, California, and St. Louis, Missouri, to bring back public flogging (hitting with a cane), a punishment not seen since 1952.

Communication Activity 27

c. *Out of the frying pan and into the fire.* A pan is used to cook with, so during the cooking process it is always on a fire or a stove. The pan is very hot, but the fire is hotter, so if a person jumps out of the pan and into the fire, he or she takes himself or herself from a bad situation to a worse situation. For example, if you quit your job because you don't make enough money, you'll go from having very little money to having no money. You have jumped out of the pan and into the fire.

d. *An idle mind is the devil's workshop.* This proverb means that a person who is not busy doing something good or useful is more likely to do something bad. For example, if a teenager is sitting around not doing his homework, his mother might reprimand him by saying "An idle mind is the devil's workshop."

Communication Activity 28

You are Shannon's medical doctor. You know that Shannon needs medical help. There is no doubt in your mind that she needs medical attention.

Communication Activity 29

Write this line on page 45: "Even if I press on my stomach, I suffer."

Communication Activity 30

Write this line on page 71: "Yes, Granddaughter, it's me."

Communication Activity 31

Topic: Health Care. You will write about health care in the past, health care in the present, and health care in the future.

Here are some possible questions and suggestions to help you write your descriptions.

1. Did/Do/Will most people receive health care?
2. Where did/do/will people receive care?
3. What did/do/will hospitals or doctors' offices look like?
4. Describe the doctors.
5. Describe the medicines.
6. Describe the diseases. Which disease(s) killed/kills/will kill most people?

Communication Activity 32

Jon Harris: You are the spokesperson for Pepsi. Your company was having this contest as a promotion for the hundred-year anniversary of Pepsi. Your company will award the winning prize of $1,000,000 to the person that wins in court. However, for the time being, your company will not get involved and does not want to say who the company thinks should receive the prize money.

Communication Activity 33

The van driver said, "My van is full of these penguins. I was supposed to take them to the zoo by 10 A.M., and I can't do that now because my van has broken down. Can you please deliver them to the zoo?"

Communication Activity 34

c. *If you fall off a horse, get right back on.* This proverb means if you don't succeed at doing something the first time, you should not be afraid to try again. For example, if I take a university course and fail it, my father or mother might say to me, "Don't be discouraged! Get right back on that horse!"

d. *All that glitters is not gold.* Gold is very shiny and expensive. However, glass is shiny, but it's not expensive. This proverb means that things aren't always as they appear. Just because something shines like gold doesn't mean it is gold. We have to look closely at things before we identify them. A person might appear to be honest but actually be dishonest, and what might seem to be a small risk to gain great rewards might actually be a pathway to danger.

Communication Activity 35

Write this line on page 71: "Anything, my child."

Communication Activity 36

You are Dennis Nixon, the father of Shannon.

Communication Activity 37

You are a parent whose daughter was killed in a motorcycle accident. She was not wearing a helmet. You want a law requiring motorcycle drivers to wear helmets to be passed so that other parents will not have to go through what you went through.

Communication Activity 38

the germ theory of diseases

Communication Activity 39

a. *One good turn deserves another.* This proverb means that you should pay back a good deed with a similar or better deed. It is used in a positive sense to mean that when someone does something nice for me, I do something nice for her in return.
b. *An eye for an eye, a tooth for a tooth.* This proverb means that what I receive, I will give. If I am treated badly, I will give bad treatment.
c. *You made your bed, now lie in it.* This proverb means that we are all responsible for our actions. If our actions have caused bad consequences, then we have to accept them.
d. *Turn the other cheek.* This proverb means that if we feel we have bee wronged, the best thing to do is to look the other way and avoid seeking revenge.

Communication Activity 40

Write this line on page 45: "What can it be?" the patient asked.

Communication Activity 41

Write this line on page 71: Tatiana looks puzzled. "You're sure?"

Communication Activity 42

Judge John P. Murphy sent Richardson to jail for 180 days. In addition, the judge ordered Richardson to put half-page announcements in local newspapers and 10 radio announcements on area radio stations to apologize for the ordeal that she had put Nitsch through. The judge gave this rationale for his decision: "The rape charges were all over the papers, but when he was exonerated, nobody hears about it." The judge thought that it was only fair that everyone should hear about what Richardson had done, just as everyone had heard what Nitsch had supposedly done.

Communication Activity 43

the Industrial Revolution

Communication Activity 44

You are a neighbor. You do not agree with the parents' ideas, but you do not like the government intruding in people's private affairs.

Communication Activity 45

e. *Don't burn bridges behind you.* Literally, this proverb means that after you cross a bridge, you shouldn't burn it, because then you can't cross over the same water again. If you quit your job and speak disrespectfully to your boss before you leave, you have burned a bridge behind you; you can't return to the same place again.

f. *You scratch my back, and I'll scratch yours.* This proverb means that if you help me, I'll help you. For example, if you need help with your English homework and I need help with my math homework, I might say, "If you scratch my back, I'll scratch yours."

Communication Activity 46

"You see, I took the penguins to the zoo, but we had change left over, so I thought I would take them to the movies now."

Communication Activity 47

Topic: Communication. You will write about communication in the past, communication in the present, and communication in the future.

Here are some possible questions to help you write your descriptions.

1. How did/do/will most people communicate with people who are not near-by?
2. Did/does/will everyone have this communication system at home?
3. How much did/does/will it cost to use this system?
4. How did/does/will this communication affect daily life?
5. What was/is/will be one benefit of the communication system?
6. What was/is/will be one disadvantage of the communication system?

Communication Activity 48

On September 28, 2000, the Food and Drug Administration approved the marketing and use of the abortion-inducing pill RU-486. The FDA put only a few restrictions on the use of the pill, including requiring doctors to determine how long the woman has been pregnant before prescribing the pill, keeping track of how often the pill isn't effective, and having the woman sign a paper agreeing to a surgical abortion if it becomes necessary.

Communication Activity 49

Daisy Garcia: You are the manager who was on duty when Allen found the bottle. Your position is that they should split the money. You are a little surprised that Allen has convinced herself that what she did isn't wrong.

Communication Activity 50

the invention of the internal combustion engine

Communication Activity 51

Write this line on page 71: "It's really, really you, Grandmother?" Tatiana repeats.

Communication Activity 52

The district attorney informed the driver that he would not be charged in the accident. Based on how the laws were written at that time, the most that officials could do would be to give him a fine of $50 and mail him two traffic tickets. The tickets would result in negative points on the driver's record immediately, but these points would not be enough to result in a suspension of his driver's license. The DA said simply, "There is no law in the state of Pennsylvania that punishes ordinary negligence behind the wheel when the result is death."

Of course the Penas were outraged. Patricia said, "He would have gotten in more trouble if he had just threatened to kill my daughter; since he really did kill her and blamed it on his cell phone, he walks away. It's all perfectly legal."

Until laws are changed, accidents resulting from cell phone use will not result in serious punishment. The Penas are working hard to get the word out about their daughter's unnecessary death and the dangers of using a cell phone while driving.

Communication Activity 53

Write this line on page 45: Stumped, the physician sent the patient to a specialist.

Communication Activity 54

You are a husband whose wife wants to have an abortion. You really want this child, so you disagree with your wife's decision to have an abortion. You are not convinced of the doctor's advice because the doctor herself said the pregnancy *could* kill your wife, not that it *would*. In other words, it's not 100 percent certain. (Your wife is in this conversation, too.)

Communication Activity 55

You are an average citizen who does not like the government interfering with your daily life. When people get a license to drive a motorcycle, they should be free to drive the motorcycle. You are against helmets and seat belts because they are examples of the government trying to run your individual life. You view this situation as government infringement.

Communication Activity 56

Joshua was stuck to the floor. While repairing a broken piggy bank, Joshua's brother spilled glue on the floor, which Joshua then accidentally stepped in. He was barefoot, so he was unable to break free of the glue until several hours later when firefighters arrived and used vegetable oil to loosen the glue.

Communication Activity 57

You are a neighbor. You do not agree with the parents' ideas. You think that their views on religion are too extreme. You believe that God gave humans minds and with these minds, we have created medicine and therefore medical help.

Communication Activity 58

e. *People who live in glass houses shouldn't throw stones.* This proverb means that you think someone is bad although he or she behaves the same way you do. If I am dishonest and my brother is dishonest, he can't say bad things about me, because I'll say, "People in glass houses shouldn't throw stones."

f. *Don't play with fire or you might get burned.* This proverb means that if you put yourself in a dangerous situation, it might have bad results. If a student repeatedly cheats on tests, his friends might say, "Don't play with fire or you might get burned."

Communication Activity 59

the discovery and harnessing of electricity

Communication Activity 60

g. *Don't close one door until you have opened another.* If you really don't like your job, it's OK to quit, but it's important to have another job before you leave your first one. If both doors are closed, you can't go anywhere.

h. *Blood is thicker than water.* Water is very thin, and blood is not. Often, we refer to our family as "blood relatives" because we share the same blood. This proverb means that family relationships are stronger than any others. If your best friend asks you for help at the same time your uncle does, you might say, "I'm sorry, but blood is thicker than water. I have to help my uncle."

Communication Activity 61

The teacher did not have to pay. The judge decided that teachers are the parents during school hours and can give "moderate correction" if it is not done with anger and does not cause permanent injury (based on a 1954 Alabama decision).

Communication Activity 62

Write this line on page 71: "Yes, I'm sure it's me."

Communication Activity 63

both world wars (World War I and World War II)

Communication Activity 64

Topic: Food. You will write about food in the past, food in the present, and food in the future.
Here are some possible questions to help you write your descriptions.

1. What food(s) did/do/will most people eat?
2. How did/do/will people get their food?
3. How did/do/will people cook or prepare the food?
4. What sorts of extra machines did/do/will people use to cook food?
5. How much time did/do/will people spend getting and preparing their food?
6. How often did/do/will people eat out?

Communication Activity 65

Rob Goldstein: You are Richardson's lawyer. You agree that your client left her drink in a public place. However, what if it had been her lunch bag? Would it have been OK for someone to open another person's lunch bag and see what was inside? No, definitely not, so why is this situation any different?

Communication Activity 66

You are a police officer who has been to many motorcycle accidents. You have seen the bodily injury and death that can result from not wearing a helmet.

Communication Activity 67

"Calm down," said the van driver. "I already did that."

Communication Activity 68

You are Lorie Nixon, the mother of Shannon.

Communication Activity 69

the American Revolution

Communication Activity 70

A jury consisting of eight people decided in favor of Richardson. The jury decided that the bottle of Pepsi belonged to Richardson, not to Allen.

Communication Activity 71

You are a priest or religious leader. Some religious people are against abortion; others support a woman's right to control her own body. You should give the opinion that you think is appropriate.

Communication Activity 72

Write this line on page 45: The man returned to his doctor the following week.

Communication Activity 73

decoding the structure of DNA

Communication Activity 74

Write this line on page 71: Tatiana goes to a psychic to contact her dear departed grandmother.

Communication Activity 75

1. F. Although the costs of incarceration are expensive (about $20,000 per year per inmate), that amounts to $600,000 to $800,000 depending on whether a person lives 30 or 40 years after sentencing. The death penalty costs about $2 million per execution.
2. F. Through the end of November 1999, 330 white people had been executed and 206 black people had been executed. However, you are much more likely to receive the death penalty if the person you murder is white than if the person you murder is black.
3. T. Thirty-eight states have the death penalty, but only 12 forbid the death penalty for those with mental retardation.
4. F. No matter what state you commit a crime in, you can still receive the federal death penalty if you break a federal (not a state) law. For example, certain acts of kidnapping in which a death occurs could receive the death penalty, regardless of what state the crime occurs in.

5. F. Delaware hanged one man in 1996, and the state of Washington conducted two hangings in the 1990s.
6. F. Velma Barfield was executed by lethal injection in North Carolina in 1984, Karla Faye Tucker was executed in Texas in 1998, and Judy Buenano was executed in Florida in 1998. There are about 43 other women on death row awaiting execution.
7. T. Some states, however, forbid the death penalty for anyone under 18.

Communication Activity 76

Darwin's publication of *The Origin of Species*

Communication Activity 77

One day a bus driver was driving his regular bus route when he saw a van that was stopped on the side of the road. The bus driver got out of his bus and asked the van driver what the problem was.

Communication Activity 78

Topic: Transportation. You will write about transportation in the past, transportation in the present, and transportation in the future.

Here are some possible questions to help you write your descriptions.

1. How did/do/will most people travel every day?
2. How did/do/will most people travel from one city to another?
3. How did/do/will most people travel from one country to another?
4. Did/Do/Will people travel to other planets?
5. What costs will be associated with each form of transportation?
6. What was/is/will be one benefit of the most common transportation system?
7. What was/is/will be one disadvantage of the most common transportation system?

Communication Activity 79

g. *Let bygones be bygones.* A bygone is something that has happened or gone by. This proverb means that we should let things in the past remain in the past. It means that it's not good to keep thinking about bad things that happened between you and someone else. It means you should forget what happened and move forward. When you want to apologize to someone for something unpleasant that happened between you, you might say, "I think we should let bygones be bygones!"

h. *It takes two to tango.* A tango is a special kind of dance that two people do. Although some dances can be done by only one person, you need two people to tango. This proverb means that one person cannot cause a problem or fight alone. For example, if someone is complaining that another person is causing a fight between them, you might say, "It takes two to tango." This would mean that you are telling your friend that the only way that there can be a fight is if BOTH parties participate. It means that if your friend does not say anything and resists any action, then there will not be a problem, because you need two people to have this kind of problem.

Communication Activity 80

You are Charles Nixon, the pastor at the church who believes in the will of God.

Communication Activity 81

You are an average citizen. You have never ridden a motorcycle. Give your REAL opinion about what you think about this law. You must be prepared to give two or three reasons to support your opinion.

Communication Activity 82

Write this line on page 71: "Yes, my dear, it's really me."

Communication Activity 83

Here is the list (in order) that was compiled by the editors of *Encyclopedia Britannica.*

1. the Industrial Revolution
2. both world wars (World War I and World War II)
3. the American Revolution
4. the discovery and harnessing of electricity
5. the French Revolution and Napoleonic Wars
6. the germ theory of diseases
7. Darwin's publication of *The Origin of Species*
8. the invention of the internal combustion engine
9. the creation of the electrical telegraph and telephone
10. decoding the structure of DNA

Communication Activity 84

An hour later the van was repaired, and the van driver drove toward the zoo. He was shocked to see the bus driver with all the penguins driving away from the zoo. He drove as quickly as he could to catch up with the bus.

Communication Activity 85

You are a woman who very much believes that it is up to each woman to control her own body. You believe abortion is only an issue because it is women who give birth. You believe that if men could get pregnant and have children, abortion would have been legalized centuries ago.

Communication Activity 86

Topic: Marriage. You will write about marriage in the past, marriage in the present, and marriage in the future.

Here are some possible questions to help you write your descriptions.

1. Did/Do/Will most people get married?
2. Why did/do/will most people get (or not get) married?
3. At what age did/do/will most people get married?
4. How did/do/will couples meet?
5. What sorts of wedding clothing and traditions will be part of the wedding ceremony?
6. How many children did/do/will a new couple have during their marriage?
7. Did/Does/Will the bride bring a dowry to the new marriage?
8. Does/Did/Will the law allow gays and lesbians to get married?

Communication Activity 87

The court convicted the Nixons (found them guilty) of involuntary manslaughter because they used prayer and not medication to treat their daughter's diabetes when they knew what the doctors had said would happen if Shannon did not receive medical attention. The Nixons were sentenced to at least two and one-half years in prison, a year more than the prosecutor requested, because Shannon was the second of their 10 children to die for the same reason.

Communication Activity 88

Write this line on page 45: "When I press my forehead with my finger, it really hurts," a patient complained to his doctor.

Communication Activity 89

Benson Lee: You are Allen's lawyer. You support your client's position of "finders keepers, losers weepers." You believe that when someone leaves something, there is a general belief that he or she doesn't want that thing any longer.

Communication Activity 90

Write this line on page 71: Soon a deep voice emanates from the psychic saying, "Granddaughter, are you there?"

Communication Activity 91

The van driver then pleaded with the bus driver and said, "I'll give you a hundred dollars to take these penguins to the zoo."

Answer Key for Language Review Exercises

Unit 1, p. 8: 1. (*various*) It was common for me before, but now I don't do it anymore. 2. *various* 3. *various* 4. *various*

Unit 2, p. 15: 1. b   2. c   3. a   4. c   5. a   6. a   7. c   8. b   9. c   10. a   11. b   12. a   13. a   14. a

Unit 3, p. 22: (These are possible answers; students' answers may vary slightly.) 1. officially stopping something for a period of time; my driver's license 2. extremely angry or shocked; *various* 3. to make something known publicly; (*various*) in the newspaper, on the Internet, tell my friends 4. carelessness; *various* 5. something that annoys you; (*various*) ants, rain 6. financial punishment; *various* 7. an extremely sad event; *various* 8. basically; *various* 9. to say you'll do something bad if you don't get what you want; *various* 10. prohibition; *various* 11. proof that something exists or is true; *various* 12. information or facts; *various* 13. a short sleep during the day; *various* 14. to not have (enough of) something; *various* 15. gone past; *various*

Unit 4, p. 29: 1. a   2. a   3. a   4. b   5. a   6. b   7. b   8. a   9. b   10. b   11. a   12. a

Unit 5, p. 37: 1. a   2. a   3. b   4. a   5. a   6. b   7. a   8. b   9. a   10. a   11. b   12. b   13. b   14. b   15. a   16. b   17. b   18. a   19. a   20. a   21. a   22. b   23. a   24. a   25. b

Unit 6, p. 42: 1. brief   2. As long as   3. flock   4. scratch   5. feather

Unit 7, p. 45: 1. c   2. f   3. b   4. e   5. a   6. d

Unit 8, p. 51: 1. a   2. b   3. a   4. a   5. a   6. b   7. b   8. b   9. a   10. b   11. b   12. a   13. b   14. b   15. b   16. a   17. b   18. b   19. a   20. b

Unit 9, p. 55: 1. b   2. d   3. e   4. f   5. a   6. c   7. i   8. g   9. j   10. h

Unit 10, p. 68: 1. convicted; inhumanely; inmate   2. confession   3. unlawful; lethal   4. drawbacks   5. consciousness   6. administer; convulsions   7. Currently; intravenously

Unit 11, p. 71: 1. b   2. d   3. e   4. g   5. f   6. c   7. a

Unit 12, p. 76: 1. a   2. b   3. b   4. a   5. b   6. a   7. a   8. a   9. a   10. a   11. b   12. a   13. a   14. b   15. a   16. a   17. b   18. a   19. a   20. a

Unit 13, p. 86: 1. commits   2. judge; sentence   3. Vandalism   4. corporal punishment; deterrent   5. acceptable; discipline   6. breaks the law; court

Unit 14, p. 97: 1. mandatory; helmets   2. discriminated   3. law; protect   4. Statistics; citizen   5. fine *or* penalty   6. safety belts; injured *Bonus question:* (Students' answers may vary.) to summarize, to give the main facts

Unit 15, p. 103: 1. b   2. a   3. a   4. a   5. a   6. a

Unit 16, p. 110: 1. c   2. e   3. g   4. h   5. i   6. k   7. l   8. j   9. f   10. d   11. b   12. a

Unit 17, p. 120: 1. h   2. g   3. i   4. f   5. j   6. e   7. k   8. d   9. l   10. c   11. m   12. b   13. n   14. a

Unit 18, p. 123: 1. d   2. g   3. j   4. b   5. h   6. c   7. f   8. a   9. e   10. i

Unit 19, p. 131: 1. a   2. a   3. a   4. b   5. b   6. b   7. a   8. b   9. b   10. b   11. b   12. a

Unit 20, p. 139: 1. e   2. d   3. f   4. c   5. l   6. b   7. h   8. a   9. j   10. i   1. k   12. g   13. m   14. n